F. SCOTT FITZGERALD

MODERN LITERATURE MONOGRAPHS
GENERAL EDITOR: Lina Mainiero

S. Y. AGNON   *Harold Fisch*
SHERWOOD ANDERSON   *Welford Dunaway Taylor*
LEONID ANDREYEV   *Josephine M. Newcombe*
ISAAC BABEL   *R. W. Hallett*
SIMONE DE BEAUVOIR   *Robert Cottrell*
SAUL BELLOW   *Brigitte Scheer-Schäzler*
BERTOLT BRECHT   *Willy Haas*
ALBERT CAMUS   *Carol Petersen*
WILLA CATHER   *Dorothy Tuck McFarland*
JOHN CHEEVER   *Samuel Coale*
COLETTE   *Robert Cottrell*
JOSEPH CONRAD   *Martin Tucker*
JULIO CORTÁZAR   *Evelyn Picon Garfield*
JOHN DOS PASSOS   *George J. Becker*
THEODORE DREISER   *James Lundquist*
FRIEDRICH DÜRRENMATT   *Armin Arnold*
T. S. ELIOT   *Joachim Seyppel*
WILLIAM FAULKNER   *Joachim Seyppel*
F. SCOTT FITZGERALD   *Rose Adrienne Gallo*
FORD MADOX FORD   *Sondra J. Stang*
MAX FRISCH   *Carol Petersen*
ROBERT FROST   *Elaine Barry*
GABRIEL GARCÍA MÁRQUEZ   *George R. McMurray*
MAKSIM GORKI   *Gerhard Habermann*
GÜNTER GRASS   *Kurt Lothar Tank*
PETER HANDKE   *Nicholas Hern*
ERNEST HEMINGWAY   *Samuel Shaw*
HERMANN HESSE   *Franz Baumer*
CHESTER HIMES   *James Lundquist*
UWE JOHNSON   *Mark Boulby*
JAMES JOYCE   *Armin Arnold*
FRANZ KAFKA   *Franz Baumer*
SINCLAIR LEWIS   *James Lundquist*
GEORG LUKÁCS   *Ehrhard Bahr and Ruth Goldschmidt Kunzer*
THOMAS MANN   *Arnold Bauer*
CARSON MCCULLERS   *Richard M. Cook*
ALBERTO MORAVIA   *Jane E. Cottrell*
VLADIMIR NABOKOV   *Donald E. Morton*
FLANNERY O'CONNOR   *Dorothy Tuck McFarland*
EUGENE O'NEILL   *Horst Frenz*
JOSÉ ORTEGA Y GASSET   *Franz Niedermayer*
GEORGE ORWELL   *Roberta Kalechofsky*
KATHERINE ANNE PORTER   *John Edward Hardy*
EZRA POUND   *Jeannette Lander*
MARCEL PROUST   *James R. Hewitt*
RAINER MARIA RILKE   *Arnold Bauer*
JEAN-PAUL SARTRE   *Liselotte Richter*

(Continued on page 166)

F. SCOTT FITZGERALD

Rose Adrienne Gallo

FREDERICK UNGAR PUBLISHING CO.
NEW YORK

Library of Congress Cataloging in Publication Data
Gallo, Rose Adrienne.
  F. Scott Fitzgerald.

  Bibliography: p.
  Includes index.
  1. Fitzgerald, Francis Scott Key, 1896–1940–
Criticism and interpretation.
PS3511.I9Z625   813'.5'2   76–15650
ISBN 0–8044–2225–7

Contents

Chronology

	York City. Engaged to Zelda Sayre.
July–September 1919	Returns to St. Paul to rewrite novel, now called *This Side of Paradise*. Manuscript accepted for publication by Scribner's.
26 March 1920	*This Side of Paradise* published.
3 April 1920	Zelda and Scott married in rectory of Saint Patrick's Cathedral in New York City.
10 September 1920	*Flappers and Philosophers* published.
26 October 1921	Daughter, Frances Scott Fitzgerald, is born in Saint Paul, Minnesota.
3 March 1922	*The Beautiful and Damned* published.
22 September 1922	*Tales of the Jazz Age* published.
20 November 1923	*The Vegetable* fails at trial run in Apollo Theater at Atlantic City, New Jersey.
April 1924–December 1926	Lives in Europe (with Zelda), mostly on the Riviera. Meets Gerald and Sara Murphy. Meets Ernest Hemingway in Dingo Bar in Paris.
10 April 1925	*The Great Gatsby* published.
26 February 1926	*All the Sad Young Men* published.
December 1926	Returns to the United States with Zelda.
January 1927	Goes to Hollywood to write film script for United Artists.

April 1928–February 1930   Frequent trips to Europe. Zelda takes ballet lessons in Paris.

April 1930–June 1930   Zelda has psychological breakdown. Hospitalized in Switzerland.

September 1931   Returns to the United States after Zelda's release from sanitarium.

September 1931–Spring 1932   Goes to Hollywood to write film script for Metro-Goldwyn-Mayer. Zelda lives near parents in Montgomery, Alabama.

February 1932–January 1934   Zelda suffers second and third breakdowns.

12 April 1934   *Tender Is the Night* published.

February 1935   Hospitalized for tuberculosis.

20 March 1935   *Taps at Reveille* published.

July 1937   Returns to Hollywood under contract to Metro-Goldwyn-Mayer. Meets Sheilah Graham.

October 1939   Begins writing *The Last Tycoon*.

21 December 1940   Dies of heart attack in Hollywood.

27 December 1940   Buried in Rockville Union Cemetery in Rockville, Maryland.

I

❧❧❧❧❧❧❧❧❧❧❧❧❧❧❧❧❧❧❧❧❧❧❧

A Drama Webbed of Dreams:
Biographical Sketch

"There never was a good biography of a novelist,"
wrote Fitzgerald. "There couldn't be. He is too many
people, if he's any good."[1] A self-protective statement, perhaps, but true to the extent that the novelist
defines his selfhood in terms of his fictive creations.
The many faces of F. Scott Fitzgerald appear in his
novels and short stories. We are asked to read Fitzgerald the way we read D. H. Lawrence, the man who
said: "One sheds one's sicknesses in books."[2] For
Fitzgerald—as for Lawrence—imagination recreated
life. And out of that artistic whole grew the legend—
for legend is where the actual and the imaginative
meet.

But, before the legend began, there was the man.
Francis Scott Fitzgerald was born on a Sunday
afternoon, 24 September 1896, in St. Paul, Minnesota.
Scott's father, Edward Fitzgerald, was a quiet southern gentleman who had come from his native Montgomery County, Maryland, after the Civil War. Mr.
Fitzgerald was a descendant on his mother's side of
two colonial American families—the Scotts and the
Keys. His most famous ancestor was Francis Scott
Key, the writer of "The Star-Spangled Banner," for
whom Scott was named. A refined, kindly man, Edward Fitzgerald was no match for the erratic, aggressive woman he married.

Mary McQuillan Fitzgerald was the oldest daughter of an Irish immigrant who had built up a lucrative wholesale grocery business in St. Paul. Mary's mother inherited a fortune of about $400,000 at her husband's death.

Because of their wealth, the McQuillans looked condescendingly upon the Fitzgeralds. Scott's mother was an eccentric—as apparently all the McQuillans were. Mrs. Fitzgerald's unusual mode of dress and often strange remarks were always to be a source of embarrassment to her son.

These conflicting family backgrounds caused the young Scott to develop what he later described as "a two cylinder inferiority complex."[3]

Scott's father, whom he deeply loved and admired, had little business acumen. After his wicker-furniture business failed, Mr. Fitzgerald was compelled to accept positions for which he was temperamentally unsuited. The family moved frequently as Mr. Fitzgerald tried unsuccessfully to provide them with a comfortable living. Grandmother McQuillan's imposing mansion on Summit Avenue—St. Paul's most exclusive residential area—became for young Scott the symbol of stability and wealth. As Mrs. Fitzgerald often observed to her husband and children, they were dependent upon McQuillan bounty for the niceties that Mr. Fitzgerald could not afford to give them.

Scott was spoiled by his mother, whose fatuous admiration for her son encouraged him to believe that his desires and needs were of paramount importance. He became so egocentric in his relationships with his friends that he was often ostracized from their activities. It was not until he was fifteen that Scott began to realize that his mother's adulation was not shared by the rest of society, and that his egotism was one of the causes of rejection by his peers.

In 1911, Aunt Annabel McQuillan provided the money to send Scott to the Newman School, a select Roman Catholic academy in Hackensack, New Jersey. At Newman, he became friendly with Father—later Monsignor—Sigourney Webster Fay, and, through him, with Shane Leslie, the Anglo-Irish author. Shane was later to help Scott publish his first novel. Until his death in 1919, Monsignor Fay was to exert a profound influence upon Scott.

In 1913, when Scott was seventeen, he matriculated at Princeton University. It was there that the Fitzgerald legend began. His clever and facile writing soon attracted the attention of fellow students, such as Edmund Wilson and John Peale Bishop, with whom he formed enduring friendships that were greatly to influence his literary career. Through these two men Scott became a member of the elite Triangle Club, a dramatic group that produced a yearly musical comedy. Scott wrote the lyrics for three consecutive yearly productions.

Scott became so involved in the Triangle Club theatricals that he failed most of his courses during his freshman year at Princeton. After a grueling summer with a private tutor, he managed to return to Princeton as a sophomore. But, because of his precarious academic standing, he was barred from active participation in Triangle Club productions.

During the Christmas vacation (1914), Scott met and fell in love with Ginevra King, a very wealthy and beautiful girl who was visiting a friend in St. Paul. Ginevra outclassed him both financially and socially. Although she carried on numerous flirtations, she was genuinely charmed by the very handsome and personable Scott. When she returned to her Lake Forest home in Chicago, he began an impassioned courtship, writing her daily letters proclaiming his love. Though

they saw each other only infrequently, Scott continued to hope that Ginevra would consent to marry
him.

But, by January 1917, they quarreled seriously,
and Ginevra terminated the relationship. In September
1918 she married William Hamilton Mitchell, an en-
sign in the air corps, in a glittering society wedding.
Scott had lost her, but he never forgot her. Ginevra
was to become the prototype of the elusive "golden
girl" who was to fire the imagination of so many of
Scott's male protagonists.

Life at Princeton, meanwhile, went on at a frenetic pace. Tapped for four university clubs, Scott
decided on the prestigious Cottage Club. He also
worked hard for the Triangle Club and *The Princeton
Tiger*. Once again his numerous extracurricular activities impeded his academic progress. He was failing in
three courses. In November of his junior year, just
before the midyear exams, he contracted malaria.
Using his illness as an excuse, he officially withdrew
from Princeton in January, insisting, however, that he
have the option to return at any time to complete the
degree requirements.

Scott became interested in the war effort during
1916 and 1917. He visited his old friend, Monsignor
Fay, who enlisted his cooperation in an undercover
scheme to promote Roman Catholicism in Russia.
Political disturbances in the U.S.S.R. forced them to
delay their departure to that country. In the mean-
time, Scott received his commission as a second lieutenant in the United States infantry (October 1917),
and was assigned to Fort Leavenworth, Kansas. Before
he was shipped overseas, the war ended.

While he was in officers' training camp, he started
his first novel. *The Romantic Egotist* was completed
by March 1918. Scott sent the manuscript to Shane
Leslie, whom he had met during the Newman days.

Leslie proofread the novel and sent it to the publishers recommending that they read it and allow Scott to go overseas believing that it would be published. In August 1918 Scribner's returned the manuscript with numerous suggestions for revision. But even after Scott revised the novel, it was rejected in October 1918. The correspondence concerning *The Romantic Egotist* occasioned the beginning of Scott's lifelong friendship with Maxwell Perkins, who was the only one of the three Scribner editors to favor publication of the novel.

But there were other compensations. Once again, Scott was in love. In June 1918 he was stationed at Camp Sheridan near Montgomery, Alabama. One night, at the Country Club of Montgomery, Scott was attracted by a golden-haired beauty who was dancing with one of his friends. Her name was Zelda Sayre, and she was to become his wife. A lively, carefree girl, Zelda reveled in dancing and flirting with the young officers at nearby Camp Sheridan. Scott was smitten. Charmed by her vivacity and daring, he became one of her coterie of admirers.

Zelda Sayre was born on 24 July 1900. She came from a highly respected family, active in Montgomery affairs since 1819. Zelda's paternal grandfather, Daniel Sayre, had been the editor of the Montgomery newspaper, *The Daily Post*. Through his marriage to Musidora Morgan, the Sayres became allied with one of Alabama's distinguished families. Musidora's brother was United States Senator John Tyler Morgan.

Zelda's maternal grandfather was Senator Willis B. Machen of Kentucky. Senator Machen's daughter, Minnie, was sent to school in Montgomery, where she later married Daniel Sayre's son, Anthony.

Zelda was the youngest of Anthony and Minnie Sayre's six children. At the time of Zelda's birth, her father, who was a lawyer, had achieved distinction as a

member (he later became president) of the State Sen-
ate. Mr. Sayre was elected Judge of the City Court of
Montgomery, serving in that office for two consecutive six-year terms. In 1909 he was appointed an
Associate Judge of the Alabama Supreme Court, an
office he held until his death in 1931.

Zelda Sayre attended the Montgomery public
schools, graduating from Sidney Lanier High School
in 1918. Very popular and versatile, Zelda was considered by her classmates to be one of the prettiest and
most vivacious girls in their circle.

Zelda was barely eighteen when she met Scott in
July 1918. But, although she favored the handsome
blond lieutenant, Zelda refused to give up her numerous other beaux. Even after Zelda fell in love with
Scott, she would not settle for a marriage that promised only romance and poverty. She wanted luxury;
and Scott would have to provide it.

Scott was discharged from the army on 14 Febru-
ary 1919, and went to New York, hoping to find a
lucrative position. He had to settle for a ninety-dollar-
a-month job with the advertising agency of Barron
Collier. Scott wrote nineteen short stories between
April and June, but was unable to sell any of them.
Finally, in June, he sold "Babes in the Woods" to *The
Smart Set* for thirty dollars:

The real blight, however, was that my story had been written in college two years before, and a dozen new ones
hadn't even drawn a personal letter. The implication was
that I was on the down-grade at twenty-two. I spent the
thirty dollars on a magenta feather fan for a girl in Alabama.[4]

But the magenta feather fan failed to pacify the
girl in Alabama who was getting nervous at Scott's
diminishing prospects of fame and fortune. When he
visited her in June 1919, Zelda broke their engage-

ment. Scott later described his return to New York: "Hating the city, I got roaring, weeping drunk on my last penny and went home. . . ."[5]

Scott returned to the family home in St. Paul, where he rewrote *The Romantic Egotist*. He completed the novel, which he now called *This Side of Paradise*, in September and submitted it to Scribner's for consideration. Within two weeks, Scribner's accepted the manuscript.

Shortly after the acceptance of *This Side of Paradise*, Scott met Harold Ober, a young literary agent at the Reynolds agency. The association with Ober, which began in November 1919, developed into a close and long-lasting friendship. It was to become strained only toward the end of Scott's life when Ober decided, regretfully, that he could not advance him any more money on stories that were not completed.

But in the fall of 1919 and the spring of 1920, Ober was selling Scott's stories to the *Saturday Evening Post* for $600. With *This Side of Paradise* in hand and the sale of several short stories, Scott visited Zelda to persuade her to resume their engagement. The engagement was announced formally on 20 March 1920, *This Side of Paradise* was published on 26 March 1920, and Zelda and Scott were married on 3 April 1920 in the rectory of Saint Patrick's Cathedral in New York City. But, despite the fairy-tale ending, Scott never forgot the bitterness of his struggle for Zelda.

This Side of Paradise was immediately acclaimed by the public. A week after publication it sold over twenty thousand copies. In 1920 alone, the novel went through nine printings and sold 41,000 copies. That same year Scott also published his first short-story collection, *Flappers and Philosophers*, and sold the film rights to "Head and Shoulders," the first of his works to be made into a motion picture.

Scott's income in 1920 was more than $18,000.

But his earnings, although substantial for that time, could not sustain the demands of their extravagant life style. Scott, already aware that Zelda had almost no financial sense, was to become acutely conscious of his own inability to handle money prudently. Just before their marriage, he had confided to a friend that Zelda was "very beautiful and very wise and very brave," but "a perfect baby." "A more irresponsible pair than we'll be," he continued, "will be hard to imagine."[6]

Scott started to write his second novel, *The Beautiful and Damned*. It was not completed. Discovering in March that Zelda was pregnant, they decided to take an extended trip to Europe from May to July 1921. In mid-August they were back in St. Paul awaiting the birth of their child. By this time Scott was thoroughly annoyed with himself because he was unable to concentrate on his writing.

Forcing himself to work on the novel, he prepared *The Beautiful and Damned* for serialization in *Metropolitan Magazine*. Meanwhile, their daughter Scottie (Frances Scott Fitzgerald) was born on 26 October 1921.

The Beautiful and Damned was published in book form on 4 March 1922. Within a year almost 50,000 copies were sold, and Warner Brothers made it into a film.

Because Zelda disliked St. Paul, finding it incredibly dull and cold, they returned to New York and rented the house at 6 Gateway Drive in Great Neck, Long Island, that provided the setting for Scott's third novel, *The Great Gatsby*.

Churning out short stories in order to pay their debts, he was able to work only sporadically on *The Great Gatsby*. By April 1924 the impulsive Fitzgeralds decided to go to France to escape the frenzied pace of life in Great Neck. They remained abroad until December 1926—a prolonged stay during which Scott continued to work on *The Great Gatsby*.

During the summer of 1924, while they were living on the French Riviera, the Fitzgeralds met Sara and Gerald Murphy, a couple whose experiences provided the inspiration for many incidents in *Tender Is the Night*. A bittersweet portrait of the relationship between the Fitzgeralds and the Murphys is presented in *Living Well Is the Best Revenge*.[7] The two couples were part of that sad legend of expatriate life in Paris and on the Riviera from 1924 to 1929.

Scott thought that he and Zelda were living "in a sort of idyllic state among everything lovely in the way of Mediterranean delights."[8] Then, in July, he discovered that Zelda's appreciation of "Mediterranean delights" included a brief but intense romance with a French aviator, Edouard Jozan. Although their own relationship appeared to be unaffected by the interlude, Scott never forgot the incident. Many years later he portrayed Jozan in *Tender Is the Night* as the handsome French mercenary, Tommy Barban.

Scott and Zelda wintered in Italy, returning to France to wait for news of the reception of *The Great Gatsby*, which was published in April 1925. A few months later Scott wrote to a friend:

Zelda and I sometimes indulge in terrible four-day rows that always start with a drinking party but we're still enormously in love and about the only truly happily married people I know.[9]

But what they saw as happiness was derived from outrageous episodes inspired by excessive drinking. During this period the couple's erratic behavior became increasingly dangerous.

One evening, when they were dining with the Murphys at a small mountain inn, Isadora Duncan,

who was sitting at the next table, began to flirt with
Scott. Flattered by her attention, he sat at her feet
while she ran her fingers through his hair. Zelda suddenly "stood up, leapt across the table, and plunged
down a long flight of stone steps." The Murphys
found her "cut and bleeding but not seriously hurt."
The outing came to an end and the Murphys went
home. Scott and Zelda followed shortly after, but,
instead of following the road, they turned up a trolley
track onto a trestle where their car stalled. Although
they knew that this area of the track was part of a
blind curve the trolley rounded at a very high speed,
the Fitzgeralds, overcome by drink, sat back in their
car and fell asleep. They were rescued the next morning by a peasant on his way to market, who carried
them to safety twenty minutes before the oncoming
trolley smashed their car to bits.[10]

In May 1925 Scott met Ernest Hemingway at
the Dingo American Bar and Restaurant in Paris. Even
before their meeting, Scott had been impressed by
Hemingway's short stories. He interested Scribner's in
Hemingway's work by writing to Maxwell Perkins
about the young American with a brilliant future.

While the Fitzgeralds were abroad, *The Great
Gatsby* was produced on Broadway in February 1926.
Warner Brothers made the novel into its first silent
film version in 1926. Fitzgerald's third short-story
collection, *All the Sad Young Men*, was also published
during this period.

Encouraged by his successes in the United States,
Scott began to think about writing a fourth novel. He
promised Perkins that he would appear in New York
with his completed manuscript under his arm. But
the frenzied straining for good times had settled into
a life style of dissipation for Scott. His depression over
his inability to write was aggravated by financial
harassments and by his concern over Zelda's poor

health. They came back to the United States in
December 1926, but Scott had failed in his resolutions
to save some money and to complete his novel before
their return. It was not until 1934 that his fourth novel
was finally to appear, after numerous changes in title,
plot, and structure, as *Tender Is the Night*.

The Fitzgeralds had come home determined to put
some order into their lives. But, by January 1927, they
were invited to Hollywood, and their good resolutions
were dissipated in a round of partying and crude
childish pranks. The script that Scott was writing,
"Lipstick," was rejected by United Artists, and he and
Zelda left Hollywood unceremoniously. In the attempt to depart undetected, they boarded the train,
dropped to the floor, and crawled on their hands and
knees until they reached their compartment.

The following year (March 1927–March 1928)
found them living in a rented mansion, Ellerslie, on
the Delaware River near Wilmington. Although Zelda
hoped that they would find tranquility in that peaceful environment, their relationship disintegrated into a
series of violent arguments. During their stay at Ellerslie, Scott renewed his Princeton associations and
started to work seriously on his novel.

A sudden decision by Zelda, however, to become
a dancer disrupted Scott's work schedule. Once again,
they set off for Paris, where Zelda studied with a
prominent ballet teacher. Zelda was now twenty-eight.
Her desire to master the technical virtuosity de-
manded of a professional dancer was beyond achievement at her age. Zelda's inflexible determination to
succeed jarred Scott's sensitivity about his own inability to concentrate. Their quarreling became increasingly bitter.

They returned to the United States and remained
at Ellerslie between September 1928 and March 1929.
Zelda continued her frenetic ballet practice, worked

on her paintings, and wrote a series of short stories.
Scott resumed his writing of *Tender Is the Night*. The
Fitzgeralds were living on advances from Scribner's
and from Scott's lucrative sale of short stories. (His
price for each story had risen to $3500 by 1927.)

Scott was drinking heavily now. He was also
continuing to alienate his dearest friends. A number of
misunderstandings strained his close friendship with
Ernest Hemingway. Zelda and Scott took their usual
mode of escape from their problems—they went
abroad.

They returned to France in March 1929, spent a
disappointing summer on the Riviera, and went on to
Paris for the winter. Zelda resumed her ballet lessons
with a frightening obsessiveness. Her failure to get
offers for dancing parts depressed her, but she refused
to admit defeat. She continued her lessons and inces-
sant practice until she suffered a total mental collapse
in April 1929.

At a psychiatric hospital in Switzerland, Zelda's
illness was diagnosed as schizophrenia. She remained
hospitalized near Geneva until she was considered well
enough to be released in September 1931. At this time
they returned to Zelda's home town of Montgomery,
where they rented a house. While Zelda, apparently
recovered from her breakdown, lived quietly near her
parents, Scott went to Hollywood to work on a script,
"Red-Headed Woman."

That November, Zelda's father, Judge Sayre,
died. A few months later Zelda had another breakdown and was admitted to the Phipps Psychiatric
Clinic of Johns Hopkins Hospital in Baltimore. So that
he and Scottie could be close to Zelda, Scott rented La
Paix, a large old house owned by his friends, the
Turnbulls, that was situated just outside of Baltimore.

While she was hospitalized, Zelda worked assidu-
ously at her novel, *Save Me the Waltz*, which was

published on 7 October 1932, a few months after she was discharged from the institution. The pattern of intermittent insanity followed by periods of lucidity was to continue until her death in a nursing home fire in 1948. Her calmer periods were marked by compulsive efforts to prove that her creative ability was equal to her husband's.

Meanwhile, Scott prepared *Tender Is the Night* for serialization in *Scribner's Magazine*. The novel was published in book form in April 1934.

In 1935, Scott, now thirty-nine, was hospitalized several times. The anxiety and guilt he felt because of Zelda's now hopeless condition, the excessive drinking, the straitened financial conditions were contributing factors to reactivating a chronic tubercular condition. When the physical symptoms subsided, Scott suffered a nervous reaction, suddenly cracking, he said, "like an old plate." He described his breakdown in *The Crack-Up*, a series of essays written in 1935.[11]

Scott made one last attempt in Hollywood. In July 1939 he accepted a six-month contract with Metro-Goldwyn-Mayer at $1000 a week. Shortly after Scott arrived in Hollywood, he met Sheilah Graham, a young British Hollywood columnist, to whom he was deeply attracted. Their romance has been poignantly described in Sheilah's book, *Beloved Infidel*.

This new relationship was turbulent at times, particularly when Scott had been drinking. But both Sheilah and Scott seemed to find some comfort in their association. Scott eased Sheilah's sense of inferiority because of her lack of formal education. Sheilah, on the other hand, gave him the love and unqualified admiration he so desperately needed to restore his self-respect.

Scott was $40,000 in debt when he went to Hollywood. In his eighteen-month affiliation with Metro-Goldwyn-Mayer, Scott earned $90,000. He

managed to pay his debts, and to provide for both
Scottie's education at Vassar and for Zelda's care.

For the most part, Scott's film scripts were not
appreciated. Disillusioned, he retired into semiseclu-
sion to write *The Last Tycoon*, his fifth and last novel,
which was unfinished at the time of his death.

Scott was in financial straits again, he was very ill
with what he described as a recurrence of tuberculosis, and he was drinking heavily. In November 1940 he
had a coronary attack, and thereafter did most of his
writing in bed. He had promised Perkins that he
would send the first draft of the novel after January
15. On December 20 he felt quite encouraged because
he had just completed the first episode of the sixth
chapter of *The Last Tycoon*. On December 21 he
suffered a second, fatal heart attack in Sheilah Graham's apartment.

Scott had always wished that he and Zelda could
be buried with his father and mother in St. Mary's
Catholic cemetery at Rockville, Maryland. He was not
allowed Roman Catholic burial, because, according to
the church regulations that pertained in 1940, Scott
"had not performed his Easter duty [received the
annual holy communion required by the church] and
his writings were undesirable." He was buried in the
small Protestant cemetery about two miles from the
Fitzgerald family plot.[12]

On 7 November 1975, "thirty-five years after the
church denied him burial in the cemetery of the
Roman Catholic Church of St. Mary's . . . Fitzgerald
was laid to rest again with liturgical ritual and literary
honors in the church cemetery." The article in *The
New York Times* continues:

Today's ritual of reinterment—the coffins were actually
moved privately on a rainy Friday three weeks ago—
brought together in death the author, who died of a heart
attack in Hollywood in December 1940 at the age of 44;

his wife Zelda, who was killed in 1948 in a fire that destroyed a mental institution where she had long been a patient, and Fitzgerald's father and mother. . . .[13]

Scott died while writing what might have been his best novel, *The Last Tycoon*. The "promise" that he had tried to develop into actuality all during his short, tortured career appeared to be on the verge of fulfillment when he was struck down. The saddest irony is that Scott, who had hoped for acclaim all his life, died believing himself to be a professional and personal failure.

It was not until 1945 that a new generation of readers "discovered" Scott's works and accepted them with an interest and appreciation unparalleled in his lifetime. The Fitzgerald revival steadily gained momentum during the 1950s and 1960s.

Today F. Scott Fitzgerald is regarded as one of America's outstanding twentieth-century writers. His present reputation justifies Stephen Vincent Benét's prophetic evaluation written in a review of *The Last Tycoon* (edited by Edmund Wilson and published posthumously in 1941):

You can take off your hats, now, gentlemen, and I think you had better. This is not a legend. This is a reputation —and, seen in perspective, it may well be one of the most secure reputations of our time.[14]

2

∿∿∿∿∿∿∿∿∿∿∿∿∿∿∿∿∿∿

An Affair of Youth:
This Side of Paradise

When *This Side of Paradise* was published in March 1920, Fitzgerald found himself a celebrity at the age of twenty-three. His brash statement to Edmund Wilson, made two years earlier, had proved to be prophetic:

I know I'll wake up some morning and find that the debutantes have made me famous over night. I really believe that no one else could have written so searchingly the story of the youth of our generation.[1]

This Side of Paradise is, without question, a searching, vivid portrait of American youth in those years preceding and following World War I. Fitzgerald presents, with rare intimacy, the turbulent emotions of his generation—a generation whose adolescent years were shaped by the war, whose coming of age coincided with that unprecedented phenomenon in American history, the Jazz Age.[2]

This Side of Paradise was acclaimed as their book by Fitzgerald's enthusiastic youthful readers. The novel dramatizes the restless groping of a generation "grown up to find all Gods dead, all wars fought, all faiths in man shaken. . . ."

Elated by his success, Fitzgerald was nonetheless uncomfortable in the new role thrust upon him by his audience:

For just a moment, before it was demonstrated that I was unable to play the role, I . . . was pushed into the position not only of spokesman for the time but of the typical product of the same moment.[3]

This statement articulates one of the chief weaknesses of the novel. Fitzgerald is both spokesman for and typical product of his time. The author of *This Side of Paradise* is too close in age to his fictional character, Amory Blaine, to do much more than present the circumstances of Amory's "picaresque ramble" through his youth and early manhood.[4] The principal concern of the novel is Amory's quest for selfhood, but Fitzgerald does not himself possess the maturity of judgment to evaluate the quality of Amory's experiences.

Amory Blaine is introduced in the first chapter as the "son of Beatrice." His father, Stephen, having sired his only son, disappears from the action until he dies, "quietly and inconspicuously," when Amory is an undergraduate at Princeton. Beatrice Blaine, the daughter of a wealthy family, is an affected woman who takes refuge from her boredom by having periodic nervous breakdowns and mild attacks of consumption. A handsome, wealthy young man, Amory is encouraged by his doting mother to indulge all his whims. At an early age, Amory "formulated his first philosophy, a code to live by, which, as near as it can be named, was a sort of aristocratic egotism."

At fifteen Amory goes to a "gentleman's school" —St. Regis in Connecticut. During his first unhappy year at school the young egotist is "universally detested" by his classmates. In his second year Amory is completely changed. He had brought to St. Regis his arrogant, conceited "Amory plus Beatrice" personality. St. Regis "had very painfully drilled Beatrice out of him and begun to lay down new and more conventional planking on the fundamental Amory."

During this period of his life Amory acquires a surrogate father—Monsignor Darcy. This jovial prelate had been one of Beatrice's suitors, "a pagan, Swinburnian young man." When Beatrice decided to marry Stephen Blaine for his social position, the "young pagan . . . had gone through a spiritual crisis, joined the Catholic Church, and was now—Monsignor Darcy." The Monsignor becomes the guiding spirit of Amory's young manhood, encouraging his desire to go to Princeton.

Amory arrives at Princeton, determined to "be one of the gods of [his] class." He becomes involved in the Triangle Club, a campus organization that produced a yearly musical comedy, and *The Daily Princetonian*, the university newspaper. Amory succeeds in his ambition to become one of the "hot cats on top" at Princeton. Neglecting his course work in the process, Amory is placed on the list of "conditioned men." Failure to pass a mathematics examination causes "his removal from the *Princetonian* board and the slaughter of his chances for the Senior Council."

Amory is also unsuccessful in his romantic involvements. His first is Isabelle Borgé, a flighty girl, for whom Amory is only one attractive man in an "unending succession of romantic interludes." Amory leaves Isabelle, realizing that she, too, had represented for him just another conquest.

Amory's next attachment is to his distant cousin, Clara Page, a beautiful young widow with two children. Monsignor Darcy asks Amory to visit Clara because she is poor and alone in the world. Amory falls in love with Clara because "she was the first fine woman he ever knew and one of the few good people who ever interested him." Clara refuses his proposal of marriage, declaring she will never marry again. "I've got my two children," she explains, "and I want them for myself."

While Amory is at Princeton, the United States becomes involved in World War I. Book One of *This Side of Paradise*, entitled "The Romantic Egotist," closes with Amory's final day at Princeton, as he prepares to leave for officer's training camp.

Book Two, "The Education of a Personage," resumes the narrative after Amory returns from service overseas. He joins two Princeton friends, Alec Connage and Tom D'Invilliers, in New York City. Amory's father has died while he is in service, leaving him very little money. Thrown on his own resources, Amory goes to work for an advertising agency. His frustration over his straitened financial situation is aggravated by two more unhappy romances.

Rosalind Connage, Alec's sister, is a lively, spoiled debutante, "who wants what she wants when she wants it." Even though Rosalind appears to love Amory, she breaks their engagement because of his poverty. "I don't want to think of pots and kitchens and brooms," Rosalind explains. "I want to worry whether my legs will get slick and brown when I swim in the summer."

Eleanor Savage, Amory's next love, is a brilliant, unstable beauty of nineteen, who recites Verlaine and Poe. Amory is bewitched by the "gorgeous clarity of her mind." Reciting poetry and discussing metaphysics, they begin to fall in love. Amory questions the sincerity of Eleanor's avowed atheism, stating that "like most intellectuals who don't find faith convenient . . . you'll yell loudly for a priest on your death-bed." Eleanor announces that she will prove herself by riding her horse over a cliff. Ten feet from the edge, she jumps from the horse who plunges over the cliff to his death. As Amory takes her home,

Eleanor sobs that she has a "crazy streak." Her mother, she explains, had gone mad when Eleanor was eleven. When Amory leaves Eleanor at her home, he realizes that his "love [had] waned, slowly with the moon."

The futility of Amory's life is redeemed by one heroic act that he performs to save his friend, Alec Connage, from disgrace. Amory is sharing a hotel suite with Alec, who brings a young woman, Jill, to his room to spend the night. Amory is in his own room when the police come to raid the suite. Amory smuggles Jill into his section of the suite and declares to the police that she is his guest. The laws against cohabitation of unmarried men and women were stringently enforced at this time (Mann Act). Amory is saved from arrest by the hotel management's wish to avoid unsavory publicity.

During this incident Amory senses the presence of two antithetical forces in the room: one is the aura of evil that broods over the three of them (Amory, Alec, and Jill); the other, is a presence, "featureless and indistinguishable, yet strangely familiar." A few days later Amory is informed of Monsignor Darcy's sudden death on the night of the hotel episode. Amory is convinced that it was the benevolent spirit of Monsignor Darcy, urging him to renounce evil, that he had sensed in the hotel room.

In *This Side of Paradise* Amory Blaine embodies the hopes, fears, struggles, aspirations of his generation. Amory is guided in his quest for selfhood by Monsignor Darcy, who urges Amory to become a "personage." The prelate makes a rather obscure distinction between a personality and a personage. A personality, he explains, is recognizable by flashy, superficial qualities that originate almost entirely in physical energy. A personality, involved in restless activity, flits from one endeavor to another. A personage, on the other hand, gathers experience. He proceeds logically, deliberately, to "the next thing," gathering "prestige and talent." Amory, the quester who hovers between a personality and a personage, must shed his undesirable "personality" traits—his overweening self-concern, his insatiable ambition.

The concluding chapters of *This Side of Paradise* deal with Amory's attempts to reform his life. In one clean sweep Amory renounces his "old ambitions [the pursuit of beauty, of literary fame] and unrealized dreams." It is "so much more important," he decides, "to be a certain sort of man." In his desire to become a personage, Amory acknowledges his consummate selfishness. By transcending that selfishness, he resolves to bring poise and balance into his life. His second attempt to "attach a positive value to life" leads to his equation of sex with evil, and his conclusion that "inseparably linked with evil was beauty. . . . Amory knew that every time he had reached toward [beauty] longingly, it had leered out at him with the grotesque face of evil."

If indeed the beautiful is evil, as Amory intimates, then the seeker of the beautiful courts his own destruction. A man who would achieve greatness, Amory decides, must abjure all manifestations of beauty, which is so often associated, he believes, "with license and indulgence." Amory's distorted apprehension of the beautiful leads him to an untenable position. On the one hand, this attitudinizing young iconoclast decrees that selfhood is contingent upon renunciation of the "beauty of great art, beauty of all joy, most of all the beauty of women"; on the other, he concedes that the essence of beauty, abstracted from its various forms, is harmony.

The contradiction rises from Amory's failure to

comprehend that selfhood cannot be achieved without the harmonious balance of the disparate elements within the human person. Amory mistakenly perceives as beautiful and desirable that which, in essence, is distorted and ugly: the insipid Isabelle, the mercenary Rosalind, the half-mad Eleanor, the licentious Jill.

In the concluding chapter of *This Side of Paradise* Amory rejects, in one grand gesture, the "generalities and epigrams" of his youth, derived from "a thousand books, a thousand lies." By the conclusion of the novel, Amory's transformation from an egotist to a personage, we are told, is complete. Fitzgerald does not reveal by what means Amory has attained the wisdom to justify his triumphant claim to self-knowledge with which the novel ends: "I know myself," Amory cries, "but that is all."

The epigraph of the novel announces that on "this side of Paradise" one finds "little comfort in the wise." For Amory's rebellious generation, Fitzgerald suggests, there is little comfort to be derived from the wisdom of their ancestors. The legacy of those wise ones consists of "old cries" and "old creeds." Wisdom, like paradise, cannot be gained by bequest, just as life cannot be lived vicariously. The wisdom that ensures selfhood must be attained by each individual by going out into "that dirty gray turmoil" of life, of experience.

One of the most perceptive studies of *This Side of Paradise* is Edmund Wilson's sharply critical analysis. The novel, he comments, is "really not *about* anything: its intellectual and moral content amounts to little more than a gesture—a gesture of indefinite revolt."[5]

In 1938, years after the book was published, Fitzgerald evaluated his first novel with commendable frankness and objectivity:

Looking it over, I think it is now one of the funniest books since 'Dorian Gray' in its utter spuriousness—and then, here and there, I find a page that is real and living."[6]

This Side of Paradise is not a good novel. Its crude, episodic structure is held together only by its central character. Unable to restrain his creative whimsy, Fitzgerald mixed a variety of genres in the book. The novel, he confessed while he was writing the first version, includes "poetry, prose, *vers libre* and every mood of a temperamental temperature."[7] One of his Princeton friends described the novel as the "collected works of F. Scott Fitzgerald published in novel form under the title of *This Side of Paradise*," adding, however, that the potpourri of almost every scrap of writing that the ebullient Fitzgerald had ever composed made "an astonishing and refreshing book."[8]

This Side of Paradise is "refreshing" because, even in its most bathetic, its most ludicrous situations, the novel compels our interest. Despite Wilson's criticism that *This Side of Paradise* "commits almost every sin a novel can possibly commit," he admitted: "it does not commit the unpardonable sin: it does not fail to live."[9]

3

~~~~~~

By Disaster Touched:
The Beautiful and Damned

The Beautiful and Damned (1922), Fitzgerald's second and least successful novel, is an ambitious attempt to explore the social and personal pressures that contribute to the disintegration of the human person. The principal victims of these corrosive forces in the novel, Anthony and Gloria Patch, are two of the usual Fitzgerald "beautiful people"—young, wealthy, and incredibly self-indulgent.

The Beautiful and Damned covers eight years in the life of Anthony Patch, "one of those many with the tastes and weaknesses of an artist with no actual creative inspiration." The novel shows "how he and his beautiful young wife are wrecked on the shoals of dissipation."[1]

Two of Anthony's friends, Richard Caramel and Maury Noble, who are first presented as men of promise, follow the same pattern of deterioration as the hapless Anthony and Gloria. Both Richard and Maury compromise their idealism by the novel's end, and succumb to the allurement of materialism.

The fate of these pitiful people is intended by Fitzgerald as an analogue for the moral and cultural debilitation of America and all of western civilization. While he was writing the novel, Fitzgerald perceived that "the greatest, gaudiest spree in history," initiated by Americans after World War I, would eventually precipitate the "death struggle of the old America,"[2] the brash, lumbering but indomitable America, quick with ingenuous faith in the illimitability of her potential.

Fitzgerald contended that foreboding of the inevitable catastrophe colored his stories of this period with "a touch of disaster." Despite his obvious identification with the fatal ebullience of his youthful protagonists, he conceded to his artistic perception. The "lovely young creatures in [his] novels went to ruin," and "his millionaires were as beautiful and damned as Hardy's peasants."[3]

The plot of *The Beautiful and Damned* is simple. It focuses upon the moral decline of Anthony Patch, who, at the age of twenty-five, directs his energies toward the attainment of his grandfather's fortune and the wooing of the beautiful siren, Gloria Gilbert. Anthony is a personable dilettante, an "exquisite dandy," who managed to graduate from Harvard with the reputation of being "a rather romantic figure, a scholar, a recluse, a tower of erudition." True to his name, Anthony is a patchwork of conflicting attitudes and unresolved aspirations. For a time he dallies, unsuccessfully, with various aesthetic pursuits. Finally, deciding upon writing as his medium of expression, he composes "some ghastly Italian sonnets, supposedly the rumination of a thirteenth-century monk on the joys of the contemplative life."

Returning to America because of his grandfather's apparently terminal illness, Anthony is thwarted in his expectations of gaining the family money when the "perpetually convalescent old man" once again recovers. Anthony settles in a luxurious New York apartment in which he enjoys an indolent, narcissistic existence on income inherited from his mother. It is at this point that the "inestimable Gloria" comes into his life. Gloria Gilbert, "the most celebrated and sought-after young beauty in the country," is more easily accessible to Anthony than the Patch millions. A lovely girl of the "most highhanded selfishness," Gloria decides to marry Anthony because she imagines that he will be content to play the "temporarily passionate lover" to her role of "permanent mistress."

The responsibilities of marriage are incomprehensible to Gloria, but she is, nonetheless, Anthony's "radiant woman," one whose unexcelled beauty is enhanced for him by her arrogant and triumphant self-assurance. Utterly engrossed in the worship of her own beauty, this "golden girl" demands that her marriage be a "live, lovely glamourous performance," in which she plays the stellar role.

The narrative follows the couple's haphazard, increasingly frustrated search for happiness from the "radiant hour" of their marriage until the "breathless idyll" begins to fade. Because Anthony and Gloria are compatible in their joint desire for graceful idleness, they are able to ignore, for a time, their essential differences. Until they begin to live beyond Anthony's income, they are sustained by romantic illusions of eternal love and beauty. Sentimentality masquerades as tenderness for these two misguided creatures; grandiose fantasies as accomplishment.

The couple purchase an old gray house in the country. Their dream is that here Anthony will write a history of the middle ages, and Gloria will be pampered by "some angelic servant still in a shadowy hinterland." Beguiled by illusion, the "passion of their pretense create[s] the actuality." But, eventually, the insubstantiality of their dreams expresses itself in the "eternal monotone: 'What then? Oh, what'll we do then?'"

A life of purposeless, monotonous ease degenerates into a ceaseless round of bacchanalian parties. Their hopes of an even more glorious future evanesce, however, on the fateful night when Grandfather Patch, ardent supporter of Prohibition, interrupts them when they are on a drunken spree. Adam Patch disinherits his grandson; Anthony and Gloria, having spent most of their money, are reduced to poverty. Unable to cope with unaccustomed deprivation, the couple's moral and physical disintegration is inexorably swift. Their attempts at reconciliation with the implacable old man are futile. When Adam Patch dies, shortly after the disastrous episode, he leaves his money to charity and reform societies. His confidant and secretary, Edward Shuttleworth, is executor of his estate and heir to a million dollars.

Anthony and Gloria contest the will. After a few years of expensive, demoralizing legal battles, which further erode their relationship, the court rules in their favor, granting them thirty million dollars. But their greed and egotism have exacted a fearful retribution. Gloria's beauty fades prematurely; Anthony suffers a complete mental collapse. The ill-starred couple sail for Europe, too debilitated to enjoy their victory.

The fate of his unhappy protagonists dramatizes the moral lesson of Fitzgerald's epigraph: "The victor belongs to the spoils." Yet, although Fitzgerald the moralist condemns their turpitude, Fitzgerald the romantic idealist mourns for beauty so recklessly squandered, so irrevocably lost. He rationalizes that "these two were marked as guilty chiefly by the freshness and fullness of their desire" for happiness.

Actually, Anthony and Gloria are damned because their perception of happiness is distorted; they mistake the illusory for the real good. Because Anthony and Gloria live in a fictive world, we can best understand the meaning of their lives by considering fully the actions through which they are defined. In *The Beautiful and Damned* Fitzgerald's treatment of these types is absorbed into the action, which is a way of saying that his characters are what they do. It is more appropriate to absorb these figures into a consideration of plot and theme rather than to present them through the conventional form of characterization based on motive and interpersonal relationships.

Fitzgerald's choice of title, *The Beautiful and Damned*, is a deliberate perversion of the platonic concept of the beautiful and good. In Plato, particularly in his *Symposium*,[4] beauty embraces redemption, for the counterpart of the beautiful is the good, and a complete perception of reality may be attained only by a synthesis of both forms. Similarly, the pursuit of happiness is motivated by love—or desire—for the beautiful and good. But Fitzgerald's title announces polarity, not synthesis. *The Beautiful and Damned* presents a grotesque distortion of a philosophical statement that directs the human person toward transcendence of the purely physical to the ultimate spiritual good.

The very movement of the novel is travesty. For, despite its emphasis upon the beautiful—the ideal to be attained and preserved at whatever cost—the prevailing atmosphere of *The Beautiful and Damned* is ugliness. The lives of the characters work downward from a perverted notion of beauty to a degree of debasement that can only be described as travesty of the platonic concept.

And the greatest travesty of all is the travesty of love. Pitiful indeed if Fitzgerald intended *The Beautiful and Damned* to be a tale of young but genuine love destroyed by external forces over which the participants have no control. Whether he realized it or not, Fitzgerald wrote a moral tale, an *exemplum*, using Anthony and Gloria as types of persons who engage in the motions of love without understanding its implications. Anthony and Gloria unite in a marriage that must ultimately fail because each brings to the relationship a consummate narcissism. Theirs is a "love" that moves toward the aggrandizement of the self instead of the happiness of the other. And it is this debasement of love that underlies the basic themes of the novel.

Anthony despises his grandfather because Adam Patch represents the old American tradition of hard work and moral righteousness that Anthony has rejected. Adam, shrewd, hard-bitten, having acquired seventy-five million dollars on the stock market, consecrates the "remainder of his life to the moral regeneration of the world." A wizened, sclerotic old man, Patch gives himself "furiously to every indignation of the age." Adam's fanaticism derives from a failure of love. It is the will to power rather than the will to love that motivates Adam Patch's reforms.

Conversely, Anthony seeks fulfillment in spurious ideals based on carefully nurtured illusions. His love for refined physical pleasures distorts his perception of happiness. Finding his female counterpart in Gloria, who concurs with Anthony's premise that life is meaningless without self-gratification, he lusts for money to satisfy his desire to be "gracefully idle." United only in their pursuit of titillating experiences, they squander their financial and emotional resources until, completely debilitated, they find themselves trapped in a meaningless way of life. This lack of purpose is first apparent in Anthony, for Gloria continues "to weave about her immeasurable illusions, immeasurable dis-

tances, immeasurable light." Her mission in life is to
give luster as her name suggests. Anthony, on the
other hand, soon perceives himself as a "futile medi-
ocrity," a little man with "copybook ambitions":

Anthony Patch with no record of achievement, without
courage, without strength to be satisfied with truth when
it was given him. Oh, he was a pretentious fool, making
careers out of cocktails and meanwhile regretting, weakly
and secretly, the collapse of an insufficient and wretched
idealism.

Gloria, who is her sole center of existence, represents the ultimate debasement of love. Her "inordinate
egotism" is, in the end, a form of self-hatred, for she
seeks to compensate for the hollowness of her inner
self by adulating her perishable physical beauty. "She
wanted to exist only as a conscious flower, prolonging
and preserving itself." Fitzgerald conceived Gloria as
the incarnation of beauty, the "susciety gurl," a type
of "bogus aristocracy."

Women, for Gloria, fall into one of two cate-
gories: clean and unclean. Uncleanness, by Gloria's
definition, indicates a variety of deficiencies in the
female person: "a lack of pride, a slackness in fibre,
and, most of all, the unmistakable aura of promiscu-
ity." It is almost impossible, concludes Gloria, for a
woman "to go downhill without a . . . cunning,
dirty sort of animality." At the end of the novel,
Gloria's beauty is tarnished. Judged by another
woman, as she (Gloria) has appraised so many others
of her sex, Gloria is described as "sort of dyed and
unclean. . . ."

Gloria's "soul and spirit were one—the beauty of
her body was the essence of her soul." The deterioration of one militates the sullying of the other. "To
preserve the integrity of her first gift [her beauty] she

had looked no more for love." Gloria's mortal physical self has become the supreme good of her life.

Such a perversion of the platonic concept of beauty must be reflected in a similar perversion of art, for art is valid only when it is seen in the broader contexts of the beautiful, the good, the true. In a world in which the desired good is conceived as power, money, egotism—art is conceived as serving a correspondingly debased purpose.

Richard Caramel, an enthusiastic, ambitious writer of meager artistic talent, experiences an instant success with his first novel, *The Demon Lover*, described as a highly original work. The title of his book recalls its lofty source in Coleridge's poem, "Kubla Khan." Richard's "overwritten piece of sustained description" stands in sorry contrast with those exquisite lines charged with the magical power of Coleridge's poetic vision.

Richard, having "swallowed" his favorite writers "whole, one after another, ideas, technic, and characters," continues to write prolifically, producing syntheses of ill-conceived generalities. In a discussion with Anthony on art, Richard argues feebly for the role of the artist as inspired interpreter of vital experiential experiences. Anthony easily convinces Richard that art, meaningless in itself, assumes meaning only insofar as it succeeds in interpreting an otherwise meaningless world. The artist, concludes Anthony, writes because it is his "mode of living."

In the world of *The Beautiful and Damned*, art serves a purely pragmatic purpose, adopting itself to the current enthusiasms until it becomes saccharine and palatable to the public taste—a bon bon, a caramel. Richard Caramel, a "natural born fetish-worshipper," contributes to the debasement of art until his name becomes a "byword of contempt."

Art ceases to be art when it fails to achieve its highest good, which is truth. On that level, truth is beauty. In the meaningless world of *The Beautiful and Damned*, art, truth, and beauty are vanquished. Once again, "the victor belongs to the spoils."

Maury Noble, who had been considered at Harvard "the most unique figure in his class, the most brilliant, the most original—smart, quiet, and among the saved," is cast by Fitzgerald as the intellectual voice of the novel. But years of dissipation have undermined Maury's nobility of spirit and dulled his perception of truth.

After a drunken carousal that horrifies even Gloria with its bestiality, she runs away from the contaminated atmosphere of her home. Concerned about Gloria's safety, Anthony and his friends follow her. The group gathers at the railroad station, at which the inebriated Maury delivers a pretentious rambling discourse on religion, literature, and philosophy.

It is difficult to determine how seriously Fitzgerald intended us to take Maury's melange of derivative, half-digested ideas. Fitzgerald believed that he had strengthened the philosophical burden of Maury's harangue by interpolating some of his own current interests and reflections.[5]

The chapter is called "Symposium." Strategically positioned in the climactic part of the novel, it is presumably its "philosophical" heart. The title refers us once again to Plato's *Symposium*, reminding us that the backdrop for Fitzgerald's pitiful creatures is the wisdom of the ages.

The platonic symposium, a convivial drinking party intended to stimulate the free exchange of ideas, is far removed from the seriocomic monologue declaimed by Maury Noble, a "shadowy and fantastic gargoyle" sitting on the roof of a shed in a railroad station under the "sardonic constellations." Maury asserts that in a purposeless universe the only wisdom is cynicism; beauty has no affinity with truth; humanity "tragic and predestined" is engaged in a "grotesque and bewildered fight with nature."

The organization of Plato's *Symposium* is a dialectic toward transcendence. Fitzgerald's book works the other way. In *The Beautiful and Damned*, the organization is a retrogressive movement toward nihilism. The chapter headings of the last section of the novel, "A Matter of Civilization," "A Matter of Aesthetics," and, finally, "No Matter," indicate that humanity's search for wisdom, truth, beauty, is futile. The final end of the quest is "no matter." An interesting play on words. In a colloquial sense, "no matter" suggests that nothing really counts. Interpreted on a spiritual level, however, the phrase implies "no substance." The end of life and love in *The Beautiful and Damned* is nothingness.

Eschatological language—which is uttered in the very title—suggests human, not divine, paradoxes. Fitzgerald's characters are damned, and the measure of their damnation is their separateness from person to person and the degrading purposes that art, love, and beauty serve.

The Beautiful and Damned is technically superior to *This Side of Paradise*. Fitzgerald's use of a tripartite structure—three books, each of which is divided into three chapters—in *The Beautiful and Damned*, is an attempt to achieve the unity of organization that is lacking in his first novel. But he fails to maintain the control suggested by the structural plan in the actual development of the details of the book.

Having achieved a popular success in *This Side of Paradise*, Fitzgerald set out to prove in his second novel that he was a thinker. Mistaking prolixity for richness and depth, he burdened *The Beautiful and Damned* with a welter of ideas that are announced rather than developed.

Yet, despite Fitzgerald's pretentious philosophical utterances, *The Beautiful and Damned* merits serious consideration. Its mistakes are those of the fledgling novelist eager to impress his readers. The youthful effusions must be pitted against the novel's unquestionable verve and brilliant evocation of its period. Fitzgerald's rare gift of rendering the atmosphere of his age compels our indulgence of his eccentricities of judgment.

The Beautiful and Damned was published on 3 March 1922. Despite its obvious flaws, the novel was appraised by most of its earliest reviewers as a genuine literary contribution.

Zelda did not appreciate, however, the "literary references and the attempt to convey a profound air of erudition."[6] Carl Van Doren objected that Fitzgerald had mixed "good poetry with indifferent moralism," but was pleased "to see signs of increasing power in his work."[7] Henry Seidel Canby, on the other hand, warned that Fitzgerald had "chosen to wallow in naturalism, to be a romantic unrestrained, and he must pay the price."[8] John Peale Bishop criticized Fitzgerald's inept handling of material essential to the story, but he conceded that "taken as a whole the book represents both in plan and execution an advance on *This Side of Paradise*."[9]

4

ᘉᗢᘉᗢᘉᗢᘉᗢᘉᗢᘉᗢᘉᗢᘉᗢᘉᗢᘉᗢᘉᗢᘉᗢᘉᗢ

Gold-hatted Lover:
The Great Gatsby

Shortly before the completion of *The Great Gatsby* in 1924, Fitzgerald explained that "the whole burden" of the novel was "the loss of those illusions that give such color to the world that you don't care whether things are true or false so long as they partake of the imagined glory."[1]

The theme of "imagined glory" is dramatized, in large part, through the experiences of Jay Gatsby, a man whose world is shaped and sustained by romantic illusions. But the lack of concern with the "true or false" of things has deeper significance for Fitzgerald than one man's unwillingness to distinguish between reality and fancy. Articulated in the novel by its narrator, Nick Carraway, indifference is presented as a moral failure—a failure of society, particularly the society of the American east to recognize the imperatives of truth and honesty and justice.

The basic plot of *The Great Gatsby* is simple and uncomplicated. Jay Gatsby, formerly James Gatz, farm boy from Minnesota, has bought a mansion in West Egg, Long Island. His objective is to reestablish his romantic association with Daisy Fay, who is now married to Tom Buchanan of East Egg. Nick Carraway, a midwesterner who has come to New York to learn the bond business, rents a cottage next to the Gatsby mansion. As Daisy's second cousin and Gatsby's

neighbor, Nick is in a strategic position to be both
observer and participant in the events that lead to
Gatsby's and Daisy's ecstatic but short-lived reunion.
Concurrent with the development of the Gatsby–
Daisy affair are Nick's relationship with Jordan Baker,
Daisy's girlhood friend, who is a well-known golf
champion, and Tom Buchanan's involvement with
Myrtle Wilson, the wife of a local, impoverished
garage owner. After Tom brutally exposes the ques-
tionable sources of Gatsby's wealth, Daisy decides to
remain with her husband. Driving Gatsby's car on the
way home to East Egg, Daisy accidentally runs down
and kills Myrtle Wilson. Completely unnerved, Daisy
speeds away. To protect her, Gatsby allows it to be
assumed that he was driving the car when the fatal
accident occurred. George Wilson, convinced that
Gatsby had been Myrtle's lover and that he had deliberately caused her death, kills Gatsby and then
shoots himself.

In an early review H. L. Mencken appraised the
plot as "no more than a glorified anecdote, and not
too probable at that."[2] But beyond the simple, melodramatic narrative of *The Great Gatsby* are larger
levels of meanings that derive from its intricate
thematic and symbolic patterns.

A contributing feature to the multiple interpretations to which the novel lends itself is the ambiguity
surrounding the character of Gatsby. In a letter to
John Peale Bishop, Fitzgerald acknowledged: ". . . you
are right about Gatsby being blurred and patchy. I
never at any one time saw him clear myself—for he
started out as one man I knew and then changed into
myself—the amalgam was never complete in my
mind."[3]

But, far from being a technical flaw, this unfo-
cused delineation gives Gatsby a universal, almost

mythic stature that a more realistically defined characterization could neither warrant nor sustain.

At the age of seventeen, James Gatz, itinerant beachcomber and former farm boy, disowned, in his imagination, the "shiftless and unsuccessful farm people" who were his biological parents. At this point the legendary Jay Gatsby "sprang from his Platonic conception of himself."

Fitzgerald makes use of "platonic conception" to indicate the most rarefied form of ideality. In his short story, "The Diamond as Big as the Ritz," he describes "a room that was like a platonic conception of the ultimate prison—ceiling, floor, and all, it was lined with an unbroken mass of diamonds . . . until . . . it dazzled the eyes with a whiteness that could be compared only with itself, beyond human wish or dream."[4]

In the novel, although Gatsby is hardly capable of articulating such a philosophical concept, he is aspiring toward nothing less than the platonic ideal of the beautiful and the good. To compensate for the sordid realities of his origin and early life, James Gatz recreates himself according to his romantic conception of the ideal man. His name change notifies us of his personal ideals: the prosaic James contracted into Jay suggests the casual intimacy of the affluent that is offset by the formalizing of Gatz into an anglicized Gatsby. It is as Jay Gatsby that he is taken under the tutelage of Dan Cody, multimillionaire miner and yachtsman. In his five years on Dan's yacht Gatsby receives a "singularly appropriate education" in debauchery and ruthlessness that serves to fill out "the vague contours of Jay Gatsby . . . to the substantiality of a man." Deprived of Dan Cody's $25,000 legacy by legal maneuvers, the penniless Gatsby drifts into the army to continue the pursuit of his dream of future glory.

In 1917 the dream is personified in the lovely
Daisy Fay to whose beautiful home Lieutenant Jay
Gatsby is brought by a "colossal accident" of wartime
socializing. Intending to "take what he could and go,"
Gatsby takes Daisy Fay one October night, and finds,
instead, that "he had committed himself to the following of a grail."

At the moment, in Louisville, when Daisy seems
willing to accept his love, Gatsby notes "that the
blocks of the sidewalk really formed a ladder and
mounted to a secret place above the trees—he could
climb to it, if he climbed alone, and once there he
could suck on the pap of life, gulp down the incomparable milk of wonder." Gatsby is aware that if he
throws in his lot with Daisy he must forfeit the freedom to range through the fantasy world he has
created: "his mind would never romp again like the
mind of God." But he hesitates only momentarily,
"listening for a moment longer to the tuning-fork that
had been struck upon a star." Then, at his kiss, Daisy
blossoms "for him like a flower and [her] incarnation
was complete." Gatsby's conception of the absolute
good becomes incarnate, for him, in the perishable
physical beauty of Daisy Fay. The name Fay (fey)
assures us that she is from the same fantasy world of
ideals from which the name Jay Gatsby derives.

The character of Gatsby functions on two levels
just as Gatsby, himself, has two names: on the one, the
naturalistic—Gatz-Gatsby is a vulgar, ostentatious
parvenu for whom money is the touchstone that trans-
forms fantasy into reality; on the other—the mythic,
Jay Gatsby is the embodiment of every man's unfulfilled aspirations.

Myth has its origins in man's need to transform
his deepest emotional urges into universal images, to fit
his individual experience into the larger contexts of
the social and metaphysical patterns of the human

race. The mythic hero is a personification of the
human consciousness, and, as such, transcends the lim-
itations of individual experience. Ordinary men con-
cede to the pressures that circumscribe human achievement, but for mythic heroes—the Jay Gatsbys—the
impossible does not exist. Gatsby truly believes that
by his fiat the past can be recaptured; the present
restructured, the future guaranteed.

Fitzgerald invests Gatsby with many of the
characteristics of the heroes of myth and romance: the
miraculous birth (he springs from his own platonic
conception) or the metamorphosis (from the un-
promising James Gatz to the fabulous Jay Gatsby);
the unknown parentage (he tells Nick he is the son of
wealthy midwesterners who are dead); the mysterious, vaguely sinister background (it is bruited about
that he is a bootlegger, a nephew to Von Hindenburg,
a cousin to the Kaiser); the acquisition of untold
wealth (he had lived in the capitals of Europe like a
"young rajah . . . collecting jewels, chiefly rubies
. . ."); and, finally, the unswerving dedication to
his quest—the attainment of Daisy Fay, the "king's
daughter, the golden girl."

Despite the satiric tone with which Fitzgerald,
through Nick Carraway, describes Gatsby's flights of
fancy, he is in obvious sympathy with Gatsby's
quixotic goal. Fitzgerald, himself, until the last few
years of his life, did not relinquish the "old dream of
being an entire man in the Goethe-Byron-Shaw tradition, with an opulent American touch, a sort of J. P.
Morgan, Topham Beauclerk and St. Francis of As-
sisi."[5]

In Jay Gatsby, Fitzgerald objectifies the visionary
side of his own divided consciousness. He was, on the
one hand, the exuberant dreamer who saw life as
purely a romantic matter; on the other, he was a
"natural idealist, a spoiled priest" who was appalled at

his hedonistic excesses.[6] Fitzgerald had been brought up a Roman Catholic, and, although he had long since rejected the doctrines of the church, he had never been completely exorcised of his attraction to its ritual and of his, perhaps, guilt-ridden awareness that in his personal life he had fallen short of its moral precepts. Fitzgerald had intended to give Gatsby a Catholic background, but, in the final revision of the novel, he deleted the Catholic elements and published them separately in a short story called "Absolution." In *The Great Gatsby* Fitzgerald uses Nick Carraway to present a moral perspective that is based upon "a sense of the fundamental decencies" rather than the more narrow doctrinal judgments of a specific religious code. It was hedonism that served as religious code in the 1920s.

The novel dramatizes the reckless profligacy of the Jazz Age, a phenomenon in American history that is without parallel. Fitzgerald, who was one of its chief exponents, claimed "credit for naming it."[7] In his own words, the Jazz Age began "about the time of the May Day riots in 1919," and, "as if reluctant to die out-moded in its bed, leaped to a spectacular death in October, 1929." Fitzgerald saw it as chiefly an affair of the young in 1922, when the "wildest of all genera-tions, the generation which had been adolescent dur-ing the confusion of the War, brusquely shouldered my contemporaries out of the way and danced into the limelight." By 1923, "their elders, tired of watch-ing the carnival with ill-concealed envy, had discovered that young liquor will take the place of young blood, and with a whoop the orgy began." It was "a whole race going hedonistic, deciding on pleasure."[8]

The Great Gatsby takes place in jazz-age New York City and its glorious adjacent playground, Long Island. Nick Carraway, the narrator and controlling consciousness of the novel, is a restless young man who has come to the east in the summer of 1922 to become a bond salesman. At this point his native midwest no longer seems "the warm center of the world," but, rather, "the ragged edge of the universe." So, for a time, Nick finds himself "simultaneously enchanted and repelled by the inexhaustible variety of life" in the east.

As narrator-character, Nick is an indispensable part of the structural scheme. Not only does he relate the action, he brings to his account an immediacy, an incisiveness of feeling, of authority, that can be conveyed only by one who has experienced, directly and indirectly, the events he reports. As character, Nick is only peripherally involved in the action proper, which is limited to those events of some several months in 1922 that lead inexorably to the novel's fatal conclusion of betrayal and death. Gatsby, Daisy, Tom, and even Jordan were essentially affected by the crucial events that occurred in the antecedent action of the novel, whereas Nick reconstructs the story from what is told to him, piecemeal, by the principals involved. Yet, Nick's role is much more important than spectator-narrator; he is moral commentator. Because Gatsby, Daisy, Tom, and Jordan appeal to Nick in varying degrees for assistance, advice, or understanding, their actions and motives are evaluated and interpreted through Nick's consciousness. This device permits Fitzgerald to manipulate his material without losing his objectivity. Nick stands as a buffer between the writer and his characters, between the writer and his readers. In fact, Nick shapes these Jazz Age figures for us.

Gatsby's story is told at two removes. First, from the viewpoint of Nick as he is experiencing the events of the summer of 1922. At this point he is a young provincial, who, through his involvement with Gatsby, discovers the nature of his own search for self-definition. "I'm thirty," he tells Jordan Baker. "I'm five years too old to lie to myself and call it honor."

Second, from the viewpoint of Nick, who, two years later, is writing a book about his association with Gatsby. In the two years since Gatsby's death, Nick has achieved the freedom of spirit to make positive judgments about the "fair and foul" of life: "No—Gatsby turned out all right at the end; it is what preyed on Gatsby, what foul dust floated in the wake of his dreams that temporarily closed out my interest in the abortive sorrows and short-winded elations of men."

Although Nick believes, for a time, that he has come east permanently, he never loses sight of his heritage. The Carraways, a prominent well-to-do midwestern family, are solidly established in the American tradition of trade and free enterprise. Nick's father operates a wholesale hardware business founded by an uncle in 1851. Nick has the saving grace both of family background and a well-defined set of moral attitudes instilled in him by his father. That Nick is convinced of the validity of these inherited values is evident in that he prefaces his book on Gatsby with his father's precepts.

The contrast between Mr. Carraway and Gatsby's father is obvious and telling. Henry C. Gatz arrives for his son's funeral on the point of collapse. As he surveys the splendor of his dead son's possessions, his grief is intermingled with "an awed pride." Having had nothing to impart to his son during his life, Gatz is impressed by the trite youthful "resolves" Gatsby had written for himself, as a boy, in a ragged copy of *Hopalong Cassidy*.

Although Nick accepts his father's suggestion that a "sense of the fundamental decencies is parcelled out unequally at birth," he also demands that everyone be aware of at least the rudimentary rules of conduct. After seeing the wanton carelessness of the Buchanans and of Jordan Baker, Nick wants the whole world to discipline itself and to be "at a sort of moral attention forever." Despite his practice of reserving judgment, Nick ultimately concludes that the conduct of the world of the east falls short of even the minimum standards of behavior.

Ironically, Gatsby, who represents everything for which Nick has "an unaffected scorn," is the only one in the end who is exempted from his revulsion. Nick, himself, does not see Gatsby clearly at first. One moment Nick finds himself under the spell of "one of those rare smiles with a quality of eternal assurance in it, that you may come across four or five times in life." The next, he sees only "an elegant young rough-neck, a year or two over thirty, whose elaborate formality of speech just missed being absurd." Yet, before Gatsby's death, Nick delivers his judgment in the only compliment he has ever paid Gatsby: "They're a rotten crowd," I shouted across the lawn. "You're worth the whole damn bunch put together." With all Nick's disapproval of Gatsby's shady associations, he realizes that only Gatsby has maintained his innocence despite his tainted wealth. It is only Gatsby who has retained a pure conviction in his "incorruptible dream." In Nick's eyes the greatness of Gatsby lies in his "heightened sensitivity to the promises of life"; his redemption in his "extraordinary gift for hope."

In direct contrast to Gatsby's idealism is Tom Buchanan, a degenerate representative of the American man of strength. Fitzgerald believed that Tom was the best character he had ever created, and one of the "three best characters in American fiction in the last twenty years."[9] A hard, aggressive man with a "body capable of enormous leverage—a cruel body," Tom expresses himself primarily in terms of physicality. When he does speak, he utters platitudes, fallacies, lies, or contemptuous indictments of human weaknesses. Nick concludes that, despite his material possessions, Tom is a disillusioned man, having reached "such an acute limited excellence at twenty-one that everything afterward savored of anticlimax." His psychological insufficiencies inspire blustering attempts to assert his superiority on such flimsy grounds as belonging to the "Nordic race." Beneath Tom's harshness and defiance Nick detects a wistful desire for approval. It is not surprising that he seeks approval where it cannot be denied—in the lowest levels of society. Tom's mistress, Myrtle Wilson, is a pathetic, vulgar woman, lacking in either social graces or intellectual capacity, but possessing a smoldering sensual vitality that responds to his sexual needs.

Tom's investigation of Gatsby is motivated less by a sense of righteousness than by a malicious impulse to destroy a superior strength that is inexplicable and therefore threatening to him. As Nick perceives it, Tom cannot understand that Gatsby's nature derives its impetus from the impalpability of an indestructible idealism. Having originally bought Daisy with the gift of a $350,000 pearl necklace, Tom maneuvers to keep her at all costs—even at the far greater cost to Gatsby of his reputation, his dreams, his life.

Tom and Daisy are what Nick terms "careless" in the strongest sense of the word: ". . . they smashed up things and creatures and then retreated back into their money or their vast carelessness, or whatever it was that kept them together, and let other people clean up the mess they had made. . . ."

Daisy, according to Nick's perception, is as

ephemeral as Tom is physical. She is a creature primarily of promises that have little hope of fulfillment, although her emotional bankruptcy is concealed by her physical beauty and vitality:

Her face was sad and lovely with bright things in it, bright eyes and a bright passionate mouth, but there was an excitement in her voice that men who had cared for her found difficult to forget: a singing compulsion, a whispered "Listen," a promise that she had done gay, exciting things just a while since and that there were gay, exciting things hovering in the next hour.

The essential Daisy is as incorporeal as that voice whispering empty promises. After a token acknowledgment of her undeniable physical beauty, Nick always notices her voice, her "low, thrilling" siren's voice that is also "artificial" and "indiscreet" and "full of money."

Watching Daisy and Gatsby's ecstatic reunion, Nick remarks:

I think that voice held him most, with its fluctuating, feverish warmth, because it couldn't be over-dreamed—that voice was a deathless song.

After Daisy decides to give up Gatsby, she becomes *just* a voice for Nick as he sadly comments that only Gatsby's

dead dream fought on . . . trying to touch what was no longer tangible, struggling unhappily, undespairingly, toward that lost voice across the room.

Daisy is a vacuous creature whose self-identity is defined by externals. She is so empty that Fitzgerald can only portray her through the qualities of another. Most important among these definitions are Tom Buchanan's hulking, brute strength, and his money and position. One of the few creative acts she has performed in her life is the replication of herself in her daughter. Daisy tells Nick that when she discovered that she had given birth to a girl, she cried: "I'm glad it's a girl. And I hope she'll be a fool—that's the best thing a girl can be in this world, a beautiful little fool." Significantly, Daisy's daughter is the only child in the novel, for, where adults are childishly irresponsible, children are superfluous.

Daisy greets Nick, on their first meeting, with a stuttering little inanity: "I'm p-paralyzed with happiness." On another occasion, this girlish spirit in a woman's alluring body dissolves into tears in Gatsby's home because she has "never seen such beautiful shirts before." After one of her dinner parties, she turns to Nick, helplessly:

'What'll we do with ourselves this afternoon?' cried Daisy, 'and the day after that, and the next thirty years?'

Before Daisy kills Myrtle Wilson, she swerves the car indecisively from Myrtle to an oncoming car, and then strikes the woman rather than risk injury to herself. In criminal denial of the consequences of her action, Daisy hides her guilt behind Gatsby's final act of devotion, leaving him to bear the onus of Myrtle's death. When Nick peers into the Buchanan home after the accident, he sees Daisy and Tom sitting together: "There was an air of natural intimacy about the picture, and anybody would have said that they were conspiring together." Their unstated conspiracy is their shared comfort in irresponsibility.

Jordan Baker, at first glance, might seem to be a more substantial person than Daisy. Her character is chiefly defined in terms of cars and sports. In actuality, she is just as hollow as her friend. Her very name is like an industrial merger. Laurence E. MacPhee has pointed out that Fitzgerald probably derived the name

from the highly romanticized advertisements of the
1920s for Jordan automobiles and Baker upholstery.[10]
The name Jordan is more often a masculine than a
feminine name. The ambiguity suggests Jordan's complicated sexual identification. Brittle, self-sufficient,
carrying herself "like a young cadet," Jordan is a
golf champion and part of the "sporting life at Ashe-
ville and Hot Springs and Palm Beach."

Nick comments that Jordan uses men only to satisfy "the demands of her hard jaunty body, avoiding
relationships with clever, shrewd men" who might
detect that beyond her "cool, insolent smile" she is
"incurably dishonest." Jordan's female qualities are
observed by Nick only when she is with Daisy, and
then in such superficial matters as their "rippling and
fluttering" dresses or their languid walk. Suggesting
that there is little distinction between Jordan and
Daisy as persons, Nick often refers to them either as a
pair, "the two young women," or in a curiously
detached manner:

Sometimes she and Miss Baker talked at once, unobtrusively
and with a bantering inconsequence that was never quite
chatter, that was as cool as their white dresses and their impersonal eyes in the absence of all desire. They were here,
and they accepted Tom and me, making only a polite
pleasant effort to entertain or to be entertained.

It is interesting that cars provide Nick with his
major insights into Jordan's personality. When Jordan
leaves a "borrowed car out in the rain with the top
down, and then lied about it," Nick remembers that
she had been suspected of cheating in her first big golf
tournament. Through her careless driving, he discovers that she conducts her life as she handles a car—
with a total disregard for anything other than her
own comfort and satisfaction. Ironically, at their final

parting, Jordan accuses Nick of being guilty of the same kind of dishonesty and carelessness in *his* conducting of their romance.

Any world in which the motions and rituals of existence are divorced from the emotions is a wasteland. The wasteland, of course, is as traditional an image in art as the hero of myth and romance. What the wasteland expresses is the fallen condition in which the hero conducts his search. And there is only a short distance between this mythic geography and Fitzgerald's wastelands of the east. The theme of spiritual enervation is revealed in two complementary forms: the desolation in physical nature and its analogue in the human spirit. The topography of the wasteland extends its contours deep into the mythic and ranges into the actual. The deprivation of the wasteland manifests itself in the physical barrenness of the land and in the spiritual impotence of its inhabitants.

Fitzgerald's notable example of the wasteland is the "valley of ashes" that lies midway between West Egg and New York City. This is a desolate area where

ashes grow like wheat into ridges and hills and grotesque gardens; where ashes take the forms of houses and chimneys and rising smoke, and finally, with a transcendent effort, of ash-gray men who move dimly and already crumbling through the powdery air.

The phrases—"grow like wheat," "take the forms of houses and chimneys," and "of ash-gray men"—depict the debasement of the most elemental human needs: sustenance, domesticity, self-identity.

Fitzgerald mentions three inhabitants of the valley of ashes: George Wilson, a "blond, spiritless, anaemic man," who is the proprietor of an unprosperous garage; his crude, sensual wife, Myrtle; and a young

Greek, Michaelis, who runs the all-night coffee shop. The restaurant is approached by "a trail of ashes," and the only car in the garage is a "dust-covered wreck of a Ford which crouched in a dim corner." When Nick first visits the garage with Tom Buchanan, he has the impression that Myrtle is "walking through her husband as if he were a ghost." Ironically, a "white ashen dust" veils "everything in the vicinity—except Myrtle." Myrtle, who hopes to escape the ash heaps through her affair with Tom, succeeds only in associating herself with the wastelands of New York City and East Egg, an association that ends in her death. Fitzgerald's point is that there is no liberation from the wasteland. That Myrtle should think money a means of release is simply a delusion that intensifies her despair. For there is no essential difference between the moneyed wastelands of New York City and Long Island and the valley of ashes.

The presiding deity of the ash heaps is symbolized by the painted eyes of an oculist's advertisement: Doctor T. J. Eckleburg's faded "blue and gigantic" eyes look out "of no face, but, instead, from a pair of enormous yellow spectacles which pass over a nonexistent nose." This grotesque relic of a long-abandoned practice is identified by George Wilson, after Myrtle's death, as the all-seeing eyes of God:

Standing behind him, Michaelis saw with a shock that he was looking at the eyes of Doctor T. J. Eckleburg, which had just emerged, pale and enormous, from the dissolving night.

'God sees everything,' repeated Wilson.
'That's an advertisement,' Michaelis assured him.

The exchange of responses is profoundly ironic. The "god" of the valley of ashes is not only a faceless nonentity whose distorted perception must be rectified by man-made lenses, but also the creation of the advertising business that is dedicated to persuasion through fallacies and exaggerations. That any deity exists who "sees" man's transgressions and despairs is, Michaelis assures George, just another advertising slogan.

Moving from the valley of ashes toward New York City, Nick has a glimpse of the "city rising up across the river in white heaps and sugar lumps all built with a wish out of non-olfactory money." The dissoluteness of the New York City wasteland is camouflaged by the sugar-coating of money. Its "first wild promise of all the mystery and beauty in the world" is belied by the depravity or demoralization of its people.

In the three principal episodes set in New York City, any attempt made by the protagonists at either communication or self-definition is abortive, producing only violence, disillusionment, frustration. Despair is the dominant feeling in the wasteland.

The first episode occurs in the apartment that Tom has provided for Myrtle. Nick attends a party there, and, every time he moves to escape the stultifying atmosphere, he becomes "entangled in some wild strident argument which pulled me back, as if with ropes, into my chair." On the same occasion, Myrtle's attempts to establish herself as Daisy's equal, or to assert her right to even mention Daisy's name, precipitate a violent argument during which Tom brutally smashes her nose.

The second episode is the luncheon with Gatsby, when Nick is introduced to the gangland world of rank corruption, murders, and executions through Meyer Wolfsheim, the man "who fixed the World Series back in 1919."

The third is the confrontation episode at the Plaza Hotel during which Tom discloses to Daisy some of the unsavory sources of Gatsby's wealth. Gatsby turns excitedly to Daisy, "denying everything, defending his name against accusations that had not been made." But with every word Daisy retreats "further and further into herself," her frightened eyes revealing that "whatever intentions, whatever courage she had had" to elope with Gatsby "were definitely gone."

The meretricious world of New York City is extended to West Egg through Gatsby's sumptuous parties. Gatsby's mansion, "a factual imitation of some Hotel de Ville in Normandy," is the setting for weekly bacchanalian rites. Once again, as with the white mirage of New York City, things are not what they seem to be. The pursuit of pleasure in the wasteland ends only in the reenactment of pain. The pervading atmosphere is chimerical and vaguely sinister as the guests "glide on through the sea-change of faces and voices and color under the constantly changing light." The fare is a caterer's triumph of salads of "harlequin designs and pastry pigs and turkeys bewitched to a dark gold." The guests conduct themselves "according to the rules of behavior associated with amusement parks," and, as one party progresses, the forced joviality is "rent asunder by dissension."

Nick later describes the West Egg world as a "night scene by El Greco," the Spanish artist noted for his genius in showing the grotesque distortions of humanity in a disturbing style with somber colors:

In the foreground four solemn men in dress suits are walking along the side-walk with a stretcher on which lies a drunken woman in a white evening dress. Her hand, which dangles over the side, sparkles cold with jewels. Gravely the men turn in at a house—the wrong house. But no one knows the woman's name, and no one cares.

The most brilliant commentary on the kind of people who accept Gatsby's hospitality is the list of guests drawn up by Nick on an old railroad timetable.

There is nothing subtle about Fitzgerald's cataloguing of names, but it renders much more effectively than pages of exposition the subhuman qualities of these representatives of the nonhuman and the superhuman, but not quite the human. Among them are the animal types: the Leeches, Doctor Civet, James B. (Rot-Gut) Ferret. Then we have the garden varieties: Clarence Endive, Ernest Lilly, Newton Orchid. Others are reminiscent of prominent figures: Mrs. Claud Roosevelt, and Cecil Roebuck. Finally, there are the Cheadles, the Ripley Snells, Mrs. Ulysses Swett, the Smirkes, and the "Catlips and the Bembergs and G. Earl Muldoon, brother to that Muldoon who afterward strangled his wife." As Nick laconically remarks: "All these people came to Gatsby's house in the summer," but, with the exception of one nameless "owl-eyed man," none of them came to Gatsby's funeral that fall.

The wasteland of East Egg is defined by the "white palaces of fashionable East Egg," so like the "whited sepulchers" of the gospels that we are asked to take them as repositories for dead men's bones. The opulent red-and-white mansion of the Buchanans adds to the sterility of the wasteland, the torments of an inferno. Again, as in so many places in the novel, the house of self-indulgence is in actuality a house of pain. The torments of infidelity, jealousy, futility, experienced by Tom and Daisy, further corrupt their already fallen natures, eventually turning them both into murderers.

One of the ways that Nick gives meaning to these bizarre doings is to contrast the life styles of the American east with the life styles of the American west. After Gatsby's death, Nick decides that his disillusionment may be an indication of the westerner's inability to adapt to the tenor and quality of eastern life:

I see now that this has been a story of the West, after all—Tom and Gatsby, Daisy and Jordan and I, were all Westerners, and perhaps we possessed some deficiency in common which made us subtly unadaptable to Eastern life.

This is a gratuitous assumption on Nick's part, for although the novel is peripherally concerned with contrasting the salutary environment of the west with the corruptive east, it is not the dissolute influence of the east that has shaped the lives of these people. Rather, Fitzgerald is careful to establish that each of them had "drifted" east in search of some panacea for the ultimate futility of their lives. Tom and Daisy and Jordan were selfish materialists long before they encountered the decadent forces of East Egg. Gatsby was a hopeless visionary at the age of seventeen when he spun out for himself "a universe of ineffable gaudiness," choosing to believe that "the rock of the world was founded securely on a fairy's wing." His first initiation into corruption was through Dan Cody, who had brought all the savage violence of the most undesirable aspects of western frontier life to the "Eastern seaboard." No facile distinctions, therefore, can be made between east and west. Yet, the novel intimates that the west, particularly the midwest, represents, for those like Nick who revere it, one of the last bastions of original Americanism.

In the last lush passages of the novel, Nick compares Gatsby's dream "of the orgiastic future" with the "last and greatest of all human dreams" which began with the Dutch sailors' first glimpse of this continent:

And as the moon rose higher the inessential houses began to melt away until gradually I became aware of the old island here that flowered once for Dutch sailors' eyes—a fresh, green breast of the new world. Its vanished trees, the trees that had made way for Gatsby's house, had once pandered in whispers to the last and greatest of all human dreams; for a transitory enchanted moment man must have held his breath in the presence of this continent, compelled into an aesthetic contemplation he neither understood nor desired, face to face for the last time in history with something commensurate to his capacity for wonder.

Fitzgerald implies, through Nick Carraway, that the myth of the American dream of a utopian world in which man may hope for equality and justice and freedom has been displaced by the prosaic, immutable realities of the development of the republic as it is recorded in American history.

The most beguiling promise of the new world was freedom from religious persecution, and the material deprivation enforced by class discrimination. The American dream was based on ambition, industry, and well-defined rules of conduct. And, so long as the dream was allied with the religious motive, the impulse toward its attainment produced men of strength and character whose success contributed to the prosperity and greatness of the nation. The increasing industrialization of the incipient years of the twentieth century, followed by the physical and psychological devastation of World War I, precipitated a radical transformation in American ideals. The consequent diminution of moral discernment was deplored by Fitzgerald as early as 1921 in *The Beautiful and Damned*.

A vitiated American dream spawned a new generation of strong men, represented by the undisciplined brute force of the Tom Buchanans, and, worse, by the unscrupulous machinations of the Meyer Wolfsheims. The amoral attitudes of the 1920s are epitomized in the novel by Gatsby's cool response to Nick's query about Wolfsheim's occupation: "He's the man who fixed the World Series back in 1919." Nick's reaction is the cry of the uninitiated few who still hold to moral principles:

The idea staggered me. . . . It never occurred to me that one man could start to play with the faith of fifty million people—with the singlemindedness of a burglar blowing a a safe.

The underprivileged and the unenlightened, like the Gatsbys, who still believe in the wondrous promise of the past, do not realize that the dream has been destroyed forever. Nick, who is much more realistic than Gatsby in this respect, warns:

'You can't repeat the past.'
'Can't repeat the past?' he cried incredulously.
'Why of course you can!'
He looked around him wildly, as if the past were lurking here in the shadow of his house, just out of reach of his hand.

The Gatsbys, with their incomparable capacity for hope, believe "in the green light, the orgiastic future that year by year recedes before us. It eluded us then, but that's no matter—tomorrow we will run faster, stretch out our arms farther. . . . And one fine morning—." But this is only the illusion, the "imagined glory," and Fitzgerald knew it all too well. The prophetic voice of the novel, Nick Carraway, predicts that, unless men root themselves once again in "the fundamental decencies," they will "beat on, boats against the current, borne back ceaselessly" in spirit, to a glorified past, that, valid for its day, has little efficacy to shape the future.

The Great Gatsby was begun in 1922 while the Fitzgeralds were living in St. Paul, Minnesota. Increasing financial pressures compelled Fitzgerald to temporarily abandon the novel during 1923 in order to devote himself to writing commercial short stories. In April 1924 Fitzgerald resumed work on the novel, discarding much of the material he had previously written. *The Great Gatsby* was completed while the Fitzgeralds were staying in the south of France.

After its publication on 10 April 1925, Fitzgerald waited apprehensively for the first reviews. He was puzzled and disappointed by the general reviewer's reaction. He wrote to Edmund Wilson that "of all the reviews, even the most enthusiastic, not one had the slightest idea what the book was about. . . ."[12]

On the other hand, he was gratified by the excellent response he received from respected authors and critics.

Gertrude Stein wrote to Fitzgerald:

You are creating the contemporary world much as Thackeray did in his *Pendennis* and *Vanity Fair* and this isn't a bad compliment. You make a modern world and a modern orgy strangely enough it was never done until you did it in *This Side of Paradise*. . . . This is as good a book and different and older and that is what one does, one does not get better but different and older and that is always a pleasure.[13]

T. S. Eliot commented:

I am not in the least influenced by your remark about myself when I say it has interested and excited me more than any new novel I have seen, either English or American, for a number of years.

When I have time I should like to write to you more fully and tell you exactly why it seems to me such a remarkable book. In fact it seems to me to be the first step that American fiction has taken since Henry James.[14]

5

Plagued by the Nightingale:
Tender Is the Night

Tender Is the Night, Fitzgerald's fourth and most ambitious novel, was his favorite among his works. Although it lacks the technical perfection generally attributed to *The Great Gatsby*, *Tender Is the Night* contains some of Fitzgerald's finest writing, and reveals an extraordinary maturity of perception of the underlying causes of human failure.

The many drafts and plans that Fitzgerald wrote for the novel indicate that his consistent intention was to show "the break-up of a fine personality . . . caused not by flabbiness but really tragic forces such as the inner conflicts of the idealist and the compromises forced upon him by circumstances." His protagonist, Dick Diver, possesses "all the talents, including especially great charm." He is, in fact, a "superman in possibilities," but he lacks the "tensile strength" of the truly great personality.[1]

Dick Diver's personal tragedy exemplifies Fitzgerald's abiding fascination with the immeasurable distance between the two worlds of the ideal and the actual. The burden of the novel is Dick's futile attempts to synthesize these two irreconcilable worlds in his personal, social, and professional relationships. One man's private agony, however, gradually assumes universal significance in *Tender Is the Night*, for Dick Diver and his circle of friends and associates also function as a microcosm of western civilization.

The novel concerns itself with a set of expatriates who congregate on the French Riviera in the postwar years between 1925 and 1929. Among these international drifters are members of the decadent European aristocracy and a number of wealthy Americans of diversified social and cultural backgrounds. Although the novel begins and ends on the French Riviera, the principal action shifts between the Riviera and Zurich, Switzerland. A fifty-page flashback fills in Dick Diver's background from 1917, when he is sent by his army superiors to complete his medical studies in Zurich, to the beginning of the action proper on the Riviera in June 1925.[2]

Dick Diver is a young American psychiatrist of great promise who, while continuing his studies in Switzerland, falls in love with Nicole Warren, a rich and beautiful mental patient. Gradually yielding to Nicole's wistful, persistent offering of herself, Dick marries her against his better professional judgment.

When the novel begins, in June 1925, Dick and Nicole have been married for six years, and are living with their two children at the Villa Diana, the luxurious home they have built on the Riviera with Nicole's money. A young actress, Rosemary Hoyt, comes with her mother, Elsie Speers, to spend a few days at nearby Gausse Beach, where Rosemary meets and becomes infatuated with Dick. As Dick gradually responds to Rosemary's overtures, Nicole begins to apprehend the situation and has two sudden violent mental seizures.

Rosemary and her mother leave the Riviera; Dick helps Nicole regain her equilibrium. During their six-year marriage Dick has developed a husband-doctor attitude toward Nicole. With each recurrence of her illness he has soothed her anxieties and brought her back to sanity by recreating for her a world in which she finds some measure of stability. After Nicole's second attack, Dick opens a clinic for wealthy mental patients in partnership with a psychiatrist friend, Dr. Franz Gregorovius. At the clinic, situated in Zurich, Dick hopes to provide Nicole with an atmosphere in which she feels secure. This venture, financed by Warren money, is encouraged by Nicole's calculating sister, Baby Warren, whose purpose is to maintain the family hold on the professional services of Doctor Diver for Nicole.

At the clinic, however, Nicole experiences another mental collapse, and causes an automobile accident that almost proves fatal to both the Divers and their children. The constant drain upon Dick's own emotional resources begins to tell, and he unconsciously seeks to free himself of Nicole's devastating, parasitic dependency.

Dick takes a leave of absence from the clinic, and contrives to see Rosemary Hoyt, who has become a highly successful Hollywood actress in the four years since their first meeting.[3] They attempt to resume their romance, but after a brief sexual encounter Dick decides to return to Zurich and Nicole. Dick's partner, Gregorovius, however, alienated by reports of Dick's increasing alchoholism and his adverse effects upon some of the patients, moves to dissolve the partnership.

Dick and Nicole return to their Riviera home, the Villa Diana. As Dick's behavior becomes noticeably erratic, Nicole regains her mental stability. She initiates a romance with Tommy Barban, a handsome soldier of fortune who has been friendly with the Divers and in love with Nicole for many years. Dick contrives to compel Nicole to assert her independence of him, and he then agrees to a divorce. After Nicole's marriage to Tommy Barban, Dick returns to the United States and drifts from one small New York town practice to another. The novel concludes with Nicole apparently cured, and Dick a professional and psychological failure.

The movement of *Tender Is the Night* is like the trickling of the sands in an hourglass. Nicole's strength accrues from the weakening of Dick's. Each of the three books of the novel is presented primarily from the point of view of one character. The variations in point of view—from Rosemary's to Dick's to Nicole's —also coincide with the shifting of the hourglass, marking the ascendancy of one character over the other.

Dick, Nicole, and Rosemary are the central characters of *Tender Is the Night*. But the novel is enriched by a host of secondary figures, insignificant in themselves, who, nonetheless, provide the vibrant emotional atmosphere in which Dick and Nicole subsist. Memorable among these minor characters are Abe North, an alcoholic musician, "who after a brilliant and precocious start had composed nothing for seven years," and his charming wife, Mary, who keeps "changing herself into this kind of person or that" in the hope of reforming her husband. After Abe is brutally beaten to death in a speakeasy, Mary becomes the Contessa di Minghetti, the wife of a Middle East potentate. She later reappears in the novel as the lesbian companion of Lady Caroline Sibley-Biers, the "wickedest woman in London."

In addition to these characters are Tommy Barban, the anarchic mercenary soldier whose charm and social graces never quite conceal his primitive brute strength of purpose and desire. There is also Baby Warren, a "tall, restless virgin" with "something wooden and onanistic about her," whose sexual energies are channeled into exploiting people who may prove useful to the Warren family. From a lower level of society are the fledgling novelist, Albert McKisco, and his wife, Violet, who constantly struggles "to make tangible to herself her shadowy position as the wife of an arriviste who had not arrived." Ironically, McKisco, with a talent only for synthesizing the ideas of the best writers of his time, becomes a successful novelist, while Abe North and Dick, both possessing natural brilliance and early promise, become notable failures.

Of the three principal characters, Dick and Nicole are fully believable persons. They command our involvement in their tormented lives. Their weaknesses and inconsistencies are pathetic reminders that the human person is, at best, a fragmented being groping toward self-realization.

Rosemary Hoyt, on the other hand, is a functional character. She holds our interest because our introduction to the Diver world is through the indiscriminating, romantic eyes of this inexperienced girl, "hovering delicately on the last edge of childhood," which is precisely the perspective that Dick wants to be seen through.

If Rosemary appears to dominate the first third of the action, leading the reader to believe that she is either the central character or an essential part of the plot, that power expresses Fitzgerald's intention of making her a "catalytic agent." Having played her provocative role, therefore, in arousing Dick's desire for an uncomplicated, carefree love, Rosemary dissolves from the main action.

The ease with which Dick becomes infatuated with Rosemary is the first indication that, although his love for Nicole is the pivotal point of his life, it has become a love of compassion, of obligation rather than a mutually enriching emotion. Drawing on the only point of reference available to her, Rosemary intuits that the Divers' love was "a rather cooled relation, and actually rather like the love of herself and her mother. When people have so much for outsiders, didn't it indicate a lack of inner intensity?" Her comparison of loves rings true to a degree: the Diver marriage is, in one aspect, a sublimated father-daughter relationship. What Rosemary cannot perceive, however, is that so much of that love, the passion that does exist between the Divers must be directed most intensely toward structuring social forms to which Nicole can relate with normality. Rosemary is unaware "that the simplicity of behavior also, the nursery-like peace and good will, the emphasis on the simpler virtues, was part of a desperate bargain with the gods and had been attained through struggles she could not have guessed at."

Rosemary's rapturous evaluation of the Divers, then, is not to be given our full credence. "You have romantic eyes," Dick cautions her at one point. The irony consists in the disparity between the realities of the Divers' lives and the effusive misconceptions of a starry-eyed girl. The Divers represent to her "the exact furthermost evolution of a class, so that most people seemed awkward beside them." Rosemary does not realize—as Dick does—that "in reality a qualitative change had already set in that was not at all apparent."

At first glance Rosemary appears to function as a foil for Nicole: Rosemary's naive romanticism contrasting with Nicole's studied sophistication. In actuality, the similarities between the two women are more notable than the contrasts. Not quite eighteen years old when she arrives on the Riviera, Rosemary is just about the same age that Nicole was when *she* met and fell in love with Dick. At this age both Rosemary and Nicole are soft, ingenuous, impressionable, but they also possess the potential and inclination to be equally hard, pragmatic, determined. Both girls emerge from institutions designed to exclude jarring experiences

(Nicole from a mental clinic; Rosemary from a convent school) to worlds that are simulations of reality.

Nicole functions with a measure of stability in an insulated world created and maintained by Dick, who also interprets her attitudes toward society.

Rosemary is drawn into the artifice of Hollywood with the success of her first motion picture, *Daddy's Girl*. Her mentor and idol is her mother, Elsie Speers, who directs her daughter's life as if she were coaching her for her next leading role:

You were brought up to work—not especially to marry. Now you've found your first nut to crack and it's a good nut—go ahead and put whatever happens down to experience. Wound yourself or him—whatever happens it can't spoil you because economically you're a boy, not a girl.

Mrs. Speers's judgment is accurate. Rosemary will never be "spoiled" as an actress. Her capacity for genuine emotional involvement with anyone other than her mother is limited. She experiences life through the rehearsed emotions of the celluloid world of motion pictures. When she begs Dick to make love to her, Rosemary realizes that she is composing the words of a script: "She was calling on things she had read, seen, dreamed through a decade of convent hours. Suddenly she knew too that it was one of her greatest roles and she flung herself into it more passionately."

Rosemary is the perennial child-woman. In her first film Rosemary is cast as Daddy's Girl, and this appears to be her *leitmotif* throughout the novel. Actually, Rosemary is, and remains, very much Mommy's Girl. With no living father as a referent, Rosemary cannot conceive male persons as *men*. Her prospective lovers are evaluated by her mother's standards and measured against the illimitable perfection of her mother's image.

Rosemary thinks she is in love with Dick; in reality, she is simply encompassing him within the love she has for her mother: "But always there was Dick. Rosemary assured the image of her mother, ever carried with her, that never, never had she known any one so nice, so thoroughly nice as Dick was that night."

At one point in their relationship Dick becomes irritated with Rosemary's constant comparisons of him with her mother: "For the first time the mention of her mother annoyed rather than amused Dick. He wanted to sweep away her mother, remove the whole affair from the nursery footing upon which Rosemary persistently established it." But the novel indicates that Rosemary never evolves beyond nursery status. After their last meeting Dick declares: "Rosemary didn't grow up. . . . It's probably better that way."

Nicole, the beautiful mad woman, is the pivotal figure of *Tender Is the Night*. A silent, withdrawn woman, she nonetheless exerts an "incalculable force" over those within her sphere of influence. Nicole is a Warren—an "American ducal family without a title" whose "very name . . . caused a psychological change in people." The Warren empire has been built on the cunning manipulation of essential industries in America. Masses of exploited laborers pay "their tithe" to Nicole. Nicole's is an external strength. Money is her power.

Like the other commodities manufactured by the Warrens, Nicole is "the product of much toil and ingenuity." Her schizophrenia has rendered her helpless until she is artfully "stitched together" by Doctor Dick Diver. Like an expensive, mechanical doll, Nicole responds to external control. A psychic mannequin, she necessarily moves in the patterns of social forms choreographed by the makers of her fate: her father, Devereux Warren; her sister, Baby; her doctor-husband-keeper, Dick; and, finally, her lover, Tommy Barban.

Nicole's schizophrenia is caused by the incestuous relationship that her father fosters, unwittingly, until he physically imposes his sexual will upon her. Nicole's unresolved feelings of complicity in that forbidding relationship emerge whenever her illness recurs. Her sense of guilt is expressed in images of blackness. After her marriage to Dick, her first schizophrenic attack coincides with the birth of her second child, her daughter Topsy. The inevitable association of girl child with guilt triggers her fantasy that the "baby is black," suggesting a satanic paternity.

Both subsequent episodes of insanity erupt in bathrooms, indicating Nicole's obsession with elimination and debasement. The first occurs after the intrusion of Rosemary, Daddy's Girl, into Nicole's marriage; the second, after the murder of the black man in the bedroom of Rosemary's hotel suite. We are witness to the second attack in which Nicole desperately attempts to wash the bloodstains from the bedspread. She babbles incoherently about being forced to wear a domino, a black hooded cloak worn at masquerades.

The imagery of blackness constantly informs the reader that Nicole's psychic life is acted out from a remote place in her past beyond the actual places and persons of her immediate life.

Dick Diver is the most complex and the most controversial character in *Tender Is the Night*. In the brilliance of his promise, he represents all that Fitzgerald, himself, hoped to be; in his fall, Dick foreshadows what Fitzgerald feared he would become.

The conflicts that will later destroy Dick are early discerned by an intellectual university companion, who warns him: "You're not a romantic philosopher—you're a scientist. Memory, face, character—especially good sense. That's going to be your trouble—judgment about yourself."

At the age of twenty-six Dick is a gifted psychiatrist with a distinguished academic record. He has arrived at this point in his career with "less Achilles' heels than would be required to equip a centipede, but with plenty—." Dick's vulnerability resides in his idealism, in his "illusions of eternal strength and health, and of the essential goodness of people." Dick admits that the price of keeping his illusions intact is "incompleteness" as a man. Even Nicole, in her madness, realizes that Dick "must touch life in order to spring from it."

Dick's essential idealism is an inheritance from his father, an unworldly clergyman who became his son's "moral guide." Mr. Diver instilled in Dick his own belief "that nothing could be superior to 'good instincts,' honor, courtesy, and courage."

When Dick, sitting in a restaurant with Nicole and Rosemary, sees a group of mothers and wives who have come to France to visit their loved ones' graves, he perceives in these women all the dignity and "maturity of an older America." Almost with an effort, Dick turns "back to his two women at the table . . . and the whole new world"—the antithetical Warren world with its new values of money and power— "in which he [now] believed."

Yet, Dick remains attached to the respected traditions in which he has been raised. Standing on one of the French battlefields of World War I, Dick mourns for the irretrievable past that was destroyed there: "All my beautiful lovely safe world blew itself up here with a great gust of high explosive love." Dick's regret is not simply for a past glorified by romantic memories, but, rather, for the passing of a culture rooted in centuries of tradition, a culture that fought inch by inch to keep its heritage intact: "This took religion and years of plenty and tremendous sureties and the exact relation that existed between the classes."

The "sureties" of Dick's upbringing inspire his intention to be "brave and kind . . . and even more than that to be loved." But Dick's need "to be loved" becomes insatiable, and later compels him to draw relentlessly upon his considerable store of natural talents and graces. Dick recklessly exerts his ability to generate excitement about things "out of proportion to their importance." He is exhilarated by his "power of arousing a fascinated and uncritical love," until he realizes the "waste and extravagance involved. He sometimes looked back with awe at the carnival of affection he had given, as a general might gaze upon a massacre he had ordered to satisfy an impersonal blood lust."

Eventually, Dick violates his own nature by giving of himself so totally to those whose admiration he woos that he is left completely sterile, committed to carrying with him "the egos of certain people, early met and early loved and to be only as complete as they were themselves complete." Dick, then, becomes a sponge assimilating all the weaknesses of the poeple he has loved and pandered to.

Disproportionate love is a perversion of love, and in *Tender Is the Night* love assumes many corruptive forms. Love becomes a dehumanizing force in the novel, because it is asked to do things it cannot do. The range of love is also unlimited in the novel, encompassing virtually all kinds of sexual behavior. Yet, whatever its manifestation, love is rendered debasing, for the most part, because of the quality of emotion the characters impart to the relationship. People use sexuality in *Tender Is the Night*, forcing it to create feelings that are usually spontaneously inspired by love.

Nicole overcomes her first fear of Dick as male
by investing him, in her mad fantasies, with soft, feline
qualities: "However, you seem quieter than the others, all soft like a big cat. I have gotten to like boys
who are rather sissies. Are you a sissy?" Her perception of Dick as a sissy persists even after their marriage. On the beach at the Riviera, Nicole hands her
husband a "curious garment" she has made for him.
Dick obediently puts it on and causes a commotion by
appearing to the various groups assembled on the
beach, "clad in transparent black lace drawers. Close
inspection revealed that actually they were lined with
flesh-colored cloth."

Fitzgerald intimated that Dick's indiscriminate
yearning for love leads him to seek it in abortive or
self-destructive relationships. Dick is attracted to "sick
women"—first to Nicole; then to the hallucinatory
artist-patient at the clinic who is rendered physically
repulsive by terminal stages of syphilis. He also enjoys
"ickle durls" as Nicole calls them: Rosemary, and later
the adolescent daughter of another woman patient at
the clinic. Finally, Dick is increasingly preoccupied
with his own children, seeking them out, "not protec-
tively, but for protection."

Abraham H. Steinberg contends that Fitzgerald
deliberately "christened his hero" with a name that
would "convey the author's contempt for softness." In
gutter slang, the expression "dick diver" suggests sexual impotence.[4] The allusions to Dick's sexual softness
draw attention to the malleability of Dick's character.
For as long as she needs him, Nicole can manipulate
Dick into becoming whatever she desires, even into an
extension of her own flawed self. There is even the
suggestion that, after ten years of Dick's care, Nicole
"is less sick than any one thinks—she only cherishes
her illness as an instrument of power."

Fitzgerald's choice of the name, Dick Diver, also directs attention to the impulsiveness with which Dick flings himself into new ventures, or even to the headstrong determination to dive into, to plumb the depths of the unknown. Dick "dives" into the abyss of Nicole's deranged mind, but his emotional involvement destroys the clear, objective vision he must maintain to cure his patient and keep himself intact.

In the character of Dick Diver, Fitzgerald dramatizes his own obsessive fear of "emotional bankruptcy," an irreversible condition that he defines as the "over extension of the flank, a burning of the candle at both ends, a call upon physical [and moral] resources [one does] not command, like a man overdrawing at his bank."[5] Dick Diver, seen through Rosemary's worshiping eyes as the "organizer of private gaiety, curator of a richly incrusted happiness," has already experienced a "lesion of enthusiasm, of vitality." Like Fitzgerald during this sad period of his life, Dick is "drawing on resources [he does] not possess;" he has been "mortgaging [himself] physically and spiritually up to the hilt."[6]

Under the constant pressure of Nicole's illness and the insidious presence of the Warren money, Dick discovers that he had "lost himself—he could not tell the hour when, or the day or the week, the month or the year." He had not married Nicole for her money, for "he had never felt more sure of himself, more thoroughly his own man, than at the time of his marriage." Yet, the Warren money had gradually eroded Dick's integrity until "he had been swallowed up like a gigolo."

In many small ways, Dick reflects, his own work as a psychiatrist had become confused with Nicole's problems, and, eventually, her money had "seemed to belittle his work." Dick finally capitulates to the se-

ductiveness of the Warren fortune when he allows
Baby Warren to provide the money for the clinic he
establishes in Zurich with Gregorovius.

By the novel's end the sands of the hourglass have
drifted down. Dick, the brilliant romantic idealist, is
vanquished, forced into emotional bankruptcy; Nicole, the flawed but wealthy pragmatist, having bat-
tened on Dick's strength and love for ten years,
emerges victorious.

The structural difficulties of *Tender Is the Night*
stem from Fitzgerald's handling of its tripartite organization (see note two). Although the traditional
third-person narrator is used throughout the novel,
each of the three parts is related principally (but not
exclusively) from the point of view of a different
character.

Book I, which takes place in June and July of
1925, introduces the Divers and their circle through
the indiscriminating point of view of Rosemary Hoyt,
who imaginatively endows the Divers' world with
glamor and romance. At this point the reader is presented with two conflicting levels of awareness: the
glowing romanticism of Rosemary's appraisal of the
Divers; the undercurrent of uneasiness generated by
consistent ominous hints that the grace and charm of
the Divers' way of life is purely superficial.

Fitzgerald's manipulation of this difficult technique is impressive, but not always successful. There
are a few instances in which Rosemary is removed
from the action. One of these is the description of
Nicole in her garden at the beginning of Chapter 6.
When Rosemary reappears on the scene, Fitzgerald
abruptly shifts to her consciousness with the awkward
transition: "To resume Rosemary's point of view it
should be said that. . . ." This double point of view is
usually successful, however, because it communicates

to the reader the same ambivalence that Dick experiences within himself.

Book II, which flashes back to Zurich in the spring of 1917, fills in the grimmer realities of the Divers' background. The circumstances are revealed that (1) lead Dick to assume the dual role of Nicole's husband and psychiatrist (2) force him to accept Warren money for the sake of Nicole and their two children (3) cause him eventually to abandon his brilliant professional prospects. The flashback follows Dick's career from 1917 to 1919, when he marries Nicole, through the six years of their marriage to the summer of 1925 when Rosemary Hoyt meets them on the Riviera. This recapitulation is accomplished in some fifty pages. The transition from the flashback to the present action is skillfully realized in a superbly drawn stream-of-consciousness passage in which Nicole telescopes the six years of their marriage, revealing their first joys, the successful sale of Dick's "little book" on psychology, their increasing use of Warren money, Nicole's serious mental relapse after the birth of her daughter, her subsequent cure, and the building of the Villa Diana.

The larger part of Book II resumes the action from the end of Book I. For the remainder of the novel Fitzgerald follows a chronological order. The events of this second part are interpreted (primarily, but, again, not exclusively) from Dick's point of view. This section is positioned strategically in the novel. Having seen Dick from the outside through the eyes of an adoring adolescent in Book I, the reader is now witness to the conflicts and struggles of the inner man. Book II limns the progressive deterioration of Dick Diver from the summer of 1925 to 1928.

Book III presents a reversal in the Divers' positions. As Dick continues to degenerate, Nicole be-

comes psychologically stronger. Fitzgerald suggests
that "the completion of his [Dick's] ruination will be
the fact that cures her—almost mystically." This last
section is seen as much as possible "through Nicole's
eyes. All Dick's stories such as are *absolutely necessary*
. . . must be told without putting in his reactions or
feelings. From now on he is a mystery man, at least to
Nicole with her guessing at the mystery."[7] The process of Dick's ruin and Nicole's growing independence
takes about a year. The novel concludes with the Divers' divorce in the summer of 1929, and Dick's lapse
into professional oblivion.

The title page of the first complete edition of the
novel (it was first serialized in four installments in
Scribner's Magazine) reads: *Tender Is the Night: A
Romance*. Both the title and the epigraph are from
Keats's "Ode to a Nightingale":

Already with thee! tender is the night . . .
. . . But here there is no light,
Save what from heaven is with the breezes blown
Through verdurous glooms and winding mossy ways.

Fitzgerald knew his Keats well. This most romantic of poets was Fitzgerald's favorite. "For awhile
after you quit Keats," he wrote to his daughter, Scottie, "all other poetry seems to be only whistling or
humming." The "Ode on a Grecian Urn" he considered "unbearably beautiful," having read it, he sup-
posed, about a hundred times, assimilating "the chime
in it and the exquisite inner mechanics. Likewise with
'The Nightingale' which I can never read through
without tears in my eyes. . . ."[8]
The relevance of the title and the epigraph has
been a critical consideration since the publication of
the novel. In fact, Fitzgerald—who had previously intended to call the novel *The Drunkard's Holiday*, then

Doctor Diver's Holiday: A Romance—had some difficulty in persuading his editor, Maxwell Perkins, about the appropriateness of changing these titles to *Tender Is the Night.*

Although the title itself was a later addition, the mood of the "Ode to a Nightingale" is part of the texture of the novel. As in the poem, the principal setting of *Tender Is the Night* is Provence. The opening sequences on the French Riviera evoke a Keatsian world of sensuous beauty and romance: the luxuriant growth of "kaleidoscopic peonies massed in pink clouds . . . and the fragile mauve-stemmed roses"; the plaintive melody of the nightingale bewitching those who are attuned to its song in the "exotic darkness" of "limpid black night[s]."

The allusions to the poem broaden in the novel to the larger implications of the myth of the nightingale and its relevance to one of the principal themes of *Tender Is the Night*—ravished sexuality and perverted love.

Ovid's *Metamorphoses* recount the tale of Philomel, who was raped by Tereus, the husband of her sister, Procne. To keep Philomel from revealing the rape, Tereus tears her tongue out by the roots and imprisons her in a lonely place. After Philomel's rescue, she and Procne avenge themselves by inviting Tereus to a banquet and serving him the flesh of his own son. Discovering the nature of their revenge, Tereus attempts to stab the two sisters. At that moment, Tereus is changed into a hoopoe, Procne to a swallow, and Philomel to a nightingale.

The similarities of the fate of Philomel to Nicole's in *Tender Is the Night* are significant: the rape— Nicole is ravished by her father; the imprisonment— Nicole is confined in a mental clinic in Zurich while her father escapes with his secret intact to the Warren home in the United States; the tearing out of the tongue—Nicole, in a sense, is rendered mute by her father's pretense that her mental derangement is caused by Nicole's fantasies of sexual advances. The notion of muteness is reinforced by frequent references to Nicole's inarticulateness throughout the novel:

At times she gave an impression of repose that was at once static and evocative. This was because she knew few words and believed in none, and in the world she was rather silent, contributing just her share of urbane humor with a precision that approached meagerness.

On the other hand, Nicole, like the nightingale, takes delight in singing. Before the incestuous episode, she used to sing to her father. During their courtship and after their marriage, Nicole sings to Dick. Nicole woos with her singing, for Nicole *is* the nightingale. Those who are seduced by her poignant sweetness are "plagued by the nightingale."

But the nightingale is only one aspect of her divided soul. The numerous references to her "low, harsh" voice, her "harsh, sweet contralto" suggest the dichotomy in Nicole's psyche; the harshness of her madness, the sweetness of her allure. Under the spell of her seductive charm—for Fitzgerald intended that Nicole "should have not merely glamor but a practically irresistible glamor"[9]—romantics, such as Dick Diver, who marries her, and Abe North, who has been "heavy, belly-frightened, with love for her for years," are bewitched into forgetting the harsh realities of her schizophrenia. Like the song of the nightingale, Nicole's music is uttered from the darkness of her emotional pain. The "plaintive anthem" of this "Darkling," to use Keats' words, finds a path to the sad hearts of men.

Having taken into account the proper title, we can consider Fitzgerald's special use of the subtitle: "A Romance." Taken together they seem either redun-

dant or contradictory. Where there is tenderness in
the night we expect romance. But Fitzgerald makes a
deeper point here by drawing on an earlier American
tradition. *Tender Is the Night* is a romance because it
attempts (as does Hawthorne's *The House of the
Seven Gables*) to "connect a bygone time with the
very present that is flitting away from us. It is a legend
prolonging itself, from an epoch now gray in the distance, down into our own broad daylight, and bring-
ing along with it some of its legendary mist. . . ."[10]

Although the prevailing mood of disenchantment,
the Keatsian setting, and lush romantic atmosphere are
evocative of the "Ode to a Nightingale," the use of the
epigraph gives us access to an even larger tradition of
myth.

Fitzgerald chose to elide the following lines from
the stanza he quotes from the "Ode to a Nightingale":

> And haply the Queen-Moon is on her throne,
> Cluster'd around by all her starry Fays.

An interesting elision, for these lines reinforce the already strong link between the elemental human situation of *Tender Is the Night* and the ancient myth of
Diana of the Wood. In Greek mythology Diana was
conceived as the moon, the ruling deity of the night.
Because she was associated, especially, with the yellow
harvest moon, Diana was revered as a fertility goddess,
patroness of the woodlands and hills, of wildlife, of
hunters and herdsmen.

In *The Golden Bough*, Sir James Frazer relates
that, in ancient times, at Diana's shrine in the sacred
grove of Nemi in Latium, there grew a certain tree
that was jealously guarded by her priest and consort,
the King of the Wood.[11] For some reason, obscured
now by numerous legends, the life of the priest-king
was bound up with the sacred tree, which, apparently,

was envisioned as the embodiment of the goddess. The King of the Wood retained his office until a stronger and craftier candidate earned the right to succeed him by violating the sacred tree and vanquishing the priest-consort in mortal combat. When we know the mythical context of the action, then we perceive the deeper implication that Fitzgerald was suggesting from the eternal triangle of husband-wife-lover. And, too, Tommy Barban's challenging of Dick and eventual winning of Nicole takes on special meaning.

The complex interrelationships of Nicole, Dick, and Tommy—whose roles as goddess, priest-consort, and challenger are suggested by associative clusters of imagery—indicate patterns of human behavior that are potentially more significant than the limited range of the literal narrative. The grim forbidding myth of Diana and her priest-consort is to be seen as the archetype for the pitiable human drama enacted by Nicole and Dick.

The description of the Divers' palatial home—the Villa Diana—built on an abutment of a cliff, bounded on two sides by the "ancient hill village of Tarmes" with its terraced gardens descending in sharp levels to a ledge seven hundred feet above the Mediterranean, is reminiscent of Frazer's description in *The Golden Bough* of one of Diana's sanctuaries. At the end of the nineteenth century, this sacred grove was the site of an "Italian palace whose terraced gardens descend steeply to the lake" [of Nemi] with two Italian villages slumbering on the ancient banks of "Diana's Mirror." In ancient times, Frazer wrote, there stood "on the northern shore of the lake, right under the precipitous cliffs on which the modern village of Nemi is perched . . . the sacred grove and sanctuary of Diana Nemorensis, or Diana of the Wood."[12] A certain tree, consecrated to Diana, was the sacred center of the sanctuary.

The Divers' garden, too, focuses around "an enormous pine, the biggest tree in the garden." This is where the Divers entertain their guests, where they distribute goodwill and hospitality, and where their "worshipers" turn their faces "up toward them . . . like the faces of poor children at a Christmas tree." Rosemary reflects "that the Villa Diana was the centre of the world. On such a stage some memorable thing was sure to happen."

In this resplendent environment, Rosemary notices the goddess-like quality of Nicole's beauty: "Her face, the face of a saint, a viking Madonna, shone through the faint motes that snowed across the candle-light, drew down its flush from the wine-colored lanterns in the pine." Rosemary also observes the sacred quality of the Divers' relationship: "She thought of them both together, heard them still singing faintly a song like rising smoke, like a hymn, very remote in time and far away."

Nicole's first recurrence of madness manifests itself at a party at the Villa Diana, and Tommy actively assumes his role as her champion when he fights a duel with Albert McKisco to defend Nicole from gossip about the nature of her illness. The duel foreshadows the crucial emotional battle for Nicole's love, in which Tommy emerges victorious over Dick, and becomes the new priest-consort of the goddess. It is noteworthy that the site of the duel is contiguous to a "grove of pines." Later, Dick will assure Tommy that Nicole is "now made of—of Georgia pine which is the hardest wood known, except lignum vitae from New Zealand."

Other images that associate Nicole with the goddess Diana are those that establish Nicole's affinity with the moon, the woods and gardens. The most obvious association of Nicole with the moon is her madness, for the moon is traditionally a symbol of insanity, lunacy.

In the acute phase of her schizophrenia, Nicole writes
to Dick an incoherent letter that concludes: "I've
thought about moonlight too. . . ." Shortly after the
Diver children entertain their guests by singing "Au
clair de la lune," Nicole has a short but violent attack
that reveals her intermittent insanity to Violet Mc-
Kisco.

In many mythologies the moon represents female
sexuality and invariably shines over romance. Interestingly, Dick, who as a psychiatrist would be expected to view Nicole from a clinical viewpoint,
emphasizes, instead, the poetic associations of Nicole
with the night and the moonlight. Her "face seemed
to have just emerged from [her hair] as if this were
the exact moment when she was coming from a wood
into clear moonlight. The unknown yielded her up;
Dick wished she had no background . . . save the night
from which she had come." Shortly after, the symbols
of night, tree, and woodland merge: "Minute by minute the sweetness drained down into her out of the
willow tree, out of the dark world."

The beautiful extended description of Nicole's
peaceful proprietary walk through every area of her
lovely multileveled garden establishes her affinity with
organic floral life. But, perhaps, the most poignant
example of her association with flowers comes after
she believes that she has captured Dick:

I can remember how I stood waiting for you in the garden
—holding all my self in my arms like a basket of flowers.
It was that to me anyhow—I thought I was sweet—waiting
to hand that basket to you.

The garden imagery, significantly, reappears
when Nicole decides to sacrifice Dick for her new
lover, Tommy. Her preparations to meet Tommy are
invested with the solemnity of religious ritual:

She bathed and anointed herself. She put on the first ankle-length dress that she had owned for many years and crossed herself reverently with Chanel Sixteen. When Tommy drove up at one o'clock she had made her person into the trimmest of gardens. How good to have things like this, to be worshiped again, to pretend to have a mystery!

The ritualistic imagery associated with Dick originates in Roman Catholic mythology. Perhaps Fitzgerald used it to suggest Dick as a "spoiled priest."[13] Dick's priestly aim is to save others through the healing power of psychiatry. His invitations to his acquaintances are extended as "apostolic gesture[s]." The smooth cloth of his coat is "like a chasuble." He goes to the rescue of those (such as Mary Minghetti and Lady Caroline Sibley-Biers) who have publicly denigrated him, and listens to their problems, nodding "gravely, looking at the stone floor, like a priest in the confessional." When he leaves the Villa Diana for the last time, Dick "raise[s] his right hand and with a papal cross he bless[es] the beach from the high terrace."

The deity that Dick worships is Nicole, who is to him "the draught in the marrow of his bones." From the moment he dedicated himself to her service, Dick's love for Nicole has been a "wild submergence of soul, a dipping of all colors into an obscuring dye. . . ." Even Dick's final defeat is a spiritual act of self-negation, conducted with dignity. His anguish at losing Nicole is intense and private. Knowing that Nicole is securely involved with Tommy, Dick tells her: "I can't do anything for you any more. I'm trying to save myself." But the priest-healer cannot save himself. Dick's tender exploration of the darkness of Nicole's soul ends in his own destruction.

Tender Is the Night is the novel with which Fitzgerald had hoped to win the acclaim of both the critics and the reading public. He had been puzzled by the discrepancy between the favorable critical reception given *The Great Gatsby* and its relatively poor sales record. For nine years after the publication of *The Great Gatsby* in 1925, Fitzgerald worked on *Tender Is the Night*, developing and refining its complex structural scheme. He intended to prove, at last, that he was "much better than any of the young Americans *without exception*." With this novel, Fitzgerald was aiming at "something really NEW in form, idea, structure— the model for the age that Joyce and Stein are searching for, that Conrad didn't find."[14]

If *Tender Is the Night* does not quite measure up to this great ambition, it is, nonetheless, an impressive achievement. The novel is a notable example of the fluid, graceful rhetoric of Fitzgerald's best writing, and in its thematic depth it surpasses even *The Great Gatsby*.

Fitzgerald waited eagerly for the first critical reviews of *Tender Is the Night*. Again he was disappointed, for, although the novel was consistently between sixth and twelfth on the bestseller lists during the period of its publication (Spring 1934), the critical reaction was so varied that John Chamberlain, critic for *The New York Times*, exclaimed that the reviews might "serve as a basis for one of those cartoons on 'Why Men Go Mad.' No two reviews were alike; no two had the same tone."[15]

Henry Seidel Canby claimed "this promising novel is promising only in its first brilliant chapters. Part way through the author loses his grip upon the theme."[16] Peter Quennell, on the other hand, believed that "the second half of the book is vivid and memorable."[17] Clifton Fadiman acknowledged "that Mr. Fitzgerald's gifts are bewilderingly varied. He has wit, grace, astonishing narrative skill. . . . His prose has polish and yet also bone and muscle. But . . . he is certainly not objective; he is both contemptuous of

and in love with his characters."[18] John Chamberlain
contended that the "study of a love affair and a marriage between doctor and mental patient . . . is as
successful a bit of writing as it must have been difficult
to create in dramatic terms. Mr. Fitzgerald set himself
an incredibly confused problem, but he draws the
lines clearly as he works the problem out in terms of
two human beings."[19]

Matthew J. Bruccoli, one of the most perceptive
of the most recent generation of Fitzgerald critics, and
author of *The Composition of Tender Is the Night:
A Study of the Manuscripts*, concludes that the major
critical problems stem from the structure of the novel:

There is a shared conviction that the many excellences of
Tender Is the Night merely indicate that it would have
been a greater achievement had Fitzgerald invented a better structure. Reading *Tender Is the Night* criticism, one
develops the feeling that Fitzgerald's commentators set special standards for him. Fitzgerald's achievements are hastily
admitted and then are used to bemoan the fact that his
work is not still better. This is not really unfair, and it is,
of course, highly complimentary to Fitzgerald.[20]

Ernest Hemingway, who had first sharply criticized Fitzgerald for his use of Sara and Gerald
Murphy in the characters of Nicole and Dick Diver,
later wrote to Maxwell Perkins:

I found Scott's "Tender Is the Night" in Cuba and read it
over. It's amazing how *excellent* much of it is. Much of it
is better than anything else he ever wrote. How I wish he
would have kept on writing. Is it really all over or will he
write again? If you write him give him my great affection.
Reading that novel much of it was so good it was frightening.[21]

6

Fable to Fantasy:
The Short Fiction

In his introduction to *The Portable F. Scott Fitzgerald*, John O'Hara acclaimed Fitzgerald as "our best novelist, one of our best novella-ists, and one of our finest writers of short stories."[1] Four collections of short stories were published in Fitzgerald's lifetime, each issued to coincide with the publication of one of his novels. *Flappers and Philosophers* (September 1920) appeared a few months after *This Side of Paradise* (March 1920); *Tales of the Jazz Age* (September 1922) followed *The Beautiful and Damned* (March 1922); *All the Sad Young Men* (February 1926) came in the year after *The Great Gatsby* (April 1925); and *Taps at Reveille* (March 1935) after *Tender Is the Night* (April 1934).

This sequence of publication proved to be a successful sales maneuver, eliciting for each collection an audience familiar with the novels. To read Fitzgerald's short stories is, in fact, to revisit the moral landscape of the novels.

One useful way to approach the stories is to group them thematically. It is perhaps best to begin with the fable, for fable leads to fantasy which is one of the prevailing subjects, as we have seen, of Fitzgerald's fiction.

"The Diamond as Big as the Ritz" (October 1921; *Smart Set*, June 1922; *Tales of the Jazz Age* 1922) is a fable about a fantasy world of limitless wealth and luxury. John T. Unger, the son of a moderately wealthy family from Hades, Missouri, is sent by his parents to St. Midas—"the most expensive and most exclusive boys' preparatory school in the world," as we might have guessed from its name, which implies the sanctification of gold.

During his second year at school, John, now eighteen, is invited by his friend, Percy Washington, to spend the summer at the Washington home in the west. As they proceed on their journey, Percy confides that not only is his father the richest man in the world but that he also owns "a diamond bigger than the Ritz-Carleton Hotel." Upon their arrival John discovers that the exquisite Washington chateau is built upon this diamond mountain—"one diamond, one cubic mile without a flaw."

John is the central intelligence through whom the incredible wealth of the Washingtons and the ultimate refinements of luxurious living enjoyed in the fantastic world of El Dorado, the Washington empire, are revealed. Although John is uninitiated in the ways of the fabulously wealthy, he is an ideal observer; his earlier training in pragmatism in his home town of Hades has made him eminently receptive to the magical power that money endows:

The simple piety prevalent in Hades [had] the earnest worship of and respect for riches as the first article of its creed—had John felt otherwise than radiantly humble before them, his parents would have turned away in horror at the blasphemy.

The "Victorian motto" over the gates of John's native town, so evocative of the ominous inscription over the entrance to Dante's inferno, suggests that Hades, Missouri, is also ruled by a satanic power—in this case, mammon or greed.

The Washington family domain, El Dorado, is described as a place of exotic beauty and unparalleled opulence. To the uninitiated, such as John, El Dorado appears to be a terrestrial paradise whose beatific center is a solid diamond mountain. As John eventually discovers, however, El Dorado is a glittering hell from which there is no escape. No one must return from this magnificent trap to disclose its location. The unfortunates who unsuspectingly venture into its forbidden territory are either imprisoned there forever or painlessly executed.

As they approach the Washington territory, John is stunned by the bizarre precautions described by Percy:

John shook his head and the wraith of a hollow laugh issued silently from his parted lips. What desperate transaction lay hidden here: What a moral expedient of a bizarre Croesus: What terrible and golden mystery? . . .

During his stay John falls in love with Percy's sister, Kismine. From her he inadvertently learns that when the family have enjoyed his company for the summer, he, like former visitors, will be put to death. But, during John's visit, one prisoner escapes from El Dorado and informs the United States government of its location. John is saved from liquidation by an unexpected air attack by a squadron of government airplanes. John and Kismine leave the besieged chateau and find shelter in a wooded spot where they can watch the battle before they make their escape.

From his vantage point John observes the climactic scene when Braddock Washington defiantly offers God the ultimate bribe, "an immense and exquisitely chiselled diamond," an advance sample, he explains, of magnificent offerings to follow. "Dull, menacing thunder" is the only response to the condescending bargaining of Braddock Washington. God refuses to accept the "sacrifice" of this prophet of materialism and save El Dorado from destruction.

The planes come to earth safely and launch their land attack on the diamond mountain and chateau. Braddock, his wife, and their son Percy, disappear into a trapdoor in the diamond mountain. As Kismine hysterically explains that the mountain is wired, John observes the total annihilation of both the besieged Washingtons and the attacking pilots. The young people are left alone in the devastated Washington empire.

When John discovers that the handfuls of gems that Kismine had taken with her are rhinestones instead of diamonds, he decides that they must return to Hades where Kismine can regale the incredulous women with stories of her diamond-studded youth. For the disillusioned John, El Dorado and Hades are merely different circles in the contemporary inferno. One is the glittering hell of fabulous wealth attained; the other, the tormented hell of wealth desired. The human spirit is vitiated by both the obsessive struggle for material possessions and the desperate desire to preserve them. As in so many Fitzgerald stories, the American dream of the pursuit of happiness has been transformed into the grasping for gold, or, in this case, for diamonds. The dream is an illusion; the diamonds are rhinestones.

"The Cut-Glass Bowl" (October 1919; *Scribner's*, June 1920; *Flappers and Philosophers* 1920) begins like a parable: "There was a rough stone age and a smooth stone age and a bronze age, and many years afterward a cut-glass age." Thus, the cut-glass age is associated with the great epochs in the development of civilization.

The cut-glass age panders to the mercurial whims of the frivolous rich whose overriding concern is to

reflect in their possessions the "dazzling light of fashion from the Back Bay to the fastnesses of the Middle
West."

Evylyn Piper, the central figure of the tale, had
once been given a cut-glass bowl by a rejected suitor.
The purpose of the gift was to stress that Evylyn, like
the bowl, was "hard, beautiful, empty, and easy to see
through." The subsequent incidents of the story
proper, however, provide no justification for this
arbitrary and cruel assessment of Evylyn Piper.

When the story begins, Evylyn is involved in an
extramarital romance with Freddy Gedney. Realizing
that she is hurting her husband Harold, Evylyn promises to terminate her illicit relationship with Freddy.
Against her wishes Freddy comes to her home to make
a final plea for her love. When Harold returns home,
unexpectedly, Gedney hides in the room with the cut-
glass bowl. His presence is revealed when he accidentally strikes the bowl, causing the ringing sound of the
fine crystal to reverberate throughout the house.
Thus, in this first incident, the bowl causes Evylyn to
lose her husband's trust and affection, and, in the
course of the following eight years of silent recrimina-
tion and rejection, her youth and beauty.

The disintegration of Evylyn's marriage and her
physical beauty is followed by a disastrous accident to
her daughter Julie. The child develops blood poison-
ing after she cuts her thumb on the cut-glass bowl. To
save her life, her hand is amputated, and Julie is left
maimed, physically and psychologically.

The climax of the story occurs eleven years later,
when Evylyn is forty-six. Her interest in life is nar-
rowed to her son, Donald, who is serving at the battle
front in World War I. When the maid announces that
she has misplaced "a long, narrow envelope that looks
like an advertisement," Evylyn knows "instinctively

and unquestionably" that the letter is from the war department, notifying her of Donald's death, and that inevitably she will find it in the cut-glass bowl.

Her fears corroborated, Evylyn stares at the glittering beauty of the "never aging, never changing" bowl, that appears to taunt her with its malevolent power:

You see, this time I didn't have to hurt you directly. I didn't bother. You know it was I who took your son away. You know how cold I am and how hard and how beautiful, because once you were just as cold and hard and beautiful.

In a frenzy Evylyn grasps the enormous, heavy bowl and staggers outside with it. She topples forward with the bowl and falls despairingly, "a still, black form," surrounded by hundreds of shimmering fragments of crystal, reflecting gleams of blue and yellow light, and "crimson edged with black."

In its destruction, the bowl achieves its ultimate triumph. Its disintegration is evidently intended to coincide with the total physical collapse (or death, the point is not clear) of Evylyn Piper. But, although Evylyn sees the bowl as an agent of disaster, no logical explanation is offered for the source of the inimical power attributed to the bowl. Furthermore, the connection between the bowl and her catastrophes is arbitrary and ultimately unconvincing. The conception of the controlling symbol is excellent, but Fitzgerald fails to provide a convincing link between the symbol and the events of the plot.

"May Day" (March 1920; *Smart Set*, July 1920; *Tales of the Jazz Age*, 1922) was written shortly after the events of 1 May 1919.[2] The opening sentence of the story conjures up a triumphal scene of great battles waged upon a heroic scale:

There had been a war fought and won and the great city of the conquering people was crossed with triumphal arches and vivid with thrown flowers of white, red, and rose.

This high-flown patriotic tone is rendered discordant by the ironic description of merchants flocking to the city to capitalize on the enormous wealth that the "victorious war" had gained for the populace. They came

with their households to taste of all the luscious feasts and witness the lavish entertainments prepared—and to buy for their women furs against the next winter and bags of golden mesh and varicolored slippers of silk and silver and rose satin and cloth of gold.

The parabolic introductory section alerts the reader that the actual historical events of May Day 1919 in New York City (with the rioting and violence by bands of demobilized soldiers who had to be forcibly restrained by police squads) described in the tale are to be interpreted on a far more universal level than the literal narrative.

Fitzgerald subtly evokes the fate of the great cities of antiquity whose inhabitants, feverishly involved in the pursuit of luxury, failed to recognize the signs of their imminent extinction.

The intrusion of a date, 1 May 1919, invites us to notice the similarity between the degeneracy of those ancient societies and the post-war decadence of New York City.

The characters, brilliantly drawn, are involved in three interweaving plots. The title, "May Day," informs us, however, that Fitzgerald's primary emphasis is upon the social atmosphere that provides the setting and motivation for the petty human relationships he describes.

Gordon Sterrett, a talented but unsuccessful artist whose failure stems from a lack of self-discipline, is involved with Jewel Hudson, a vulgar adventurer from the lower classes. Gordon's friend, Philip Dean, a wealthy, self-indulgent man, refuses to lend Gordon enough money to terminate the compromising liaison with Jewel. At a party, to which Philip has invited him, Gordon meets an old flame, Edith Bradin. Edith is a vapid *femme fatale*, whose revived interest in Gordon Sterrett rapidly dissipates when she realizes that he is no longer a carefree, lighthearted companion.

Gus Rose and Carroll Key, two recently discharged soldiers, are functional characters, loosely related to the main events of "May Day." In search of amusement and liquor, they stumble into the situations that form the basis for the three major plots.

Henry Bradin, Edith's brother, is a pacifist who has left his position as instructor of economics at Cornell to run a socialist weekly newspaper in New York City. The climactic episode of "May Day" occurs when Edith impulsively decides to leave the party at Delmonico's and visit her brother's newspaper office. The building is suddenly stormed by a horde of drunken demobilized soldiers, among them Gus Rose and Carroll Key. In the melée, Carroll is accidentally shoved out the window and killed. Harry Bradin, idealist and friend to the common man, is physically assaulted by the mob and suffers a broken leg.

This apparently extraneous incident is linked to the other plots by the presence of Edith Bradin and the two soldiers, Gus and Carroll. But, more important, it serves thematically to underscore the rebellious attitude of post-war Americans of all social levels.

This violent occurrence is echoed in the morning hours after May Day in the brawl that takes place at Child's restaurant to which most of the principal characters have gone after their various traumatic experiences of the previous night.

Gordon Sterrett, intoxicated to the point of incompetency, is adroitly manipulated by Jewel Hudson, who is determined to achieve social respectability through him. When Philip Dean and Peter Himmel, drunk from the party at Delmonico's, waggishly attempt to rescue Gordon from her, Jewel marshals her prey out of the restaurant. Dean and Himmel then engage in a hash-slinging attack upon the waiters before they are evicted by the bouncer. This depressing episode concludes the May Day festivities. In ironic contrast to the sordid activities within the restaurant, the "magical, breathless dawn" arises in New York City.

"May Day" ends as it began with Gordon Sterrett, who wakes up from a drunken stupor the next morning to find himself married to Jewel Hudson. Unable to face the rest of his meaningless life, Gordon commits suicide by firing a bullet into his temple. Gordon Sterrett is the only person in "May Day" who acknowledges the futility of his life and brings it to a despairing conclusion. The other characters, for the most part, seek to submerge their demoralization by clutching at the fleeting respite promised by the mindless hedonism of the post-war era.

"May Day" is one of Fitzgerald's finest short works, foreshadowing the maturity of vision and technical dexterity of *The Great Gatsby*.

In "Winter Dreams" and "Absolution," both written before *The Great Gatsby* (1925), Fitzgerald introduced the theme (later developed in the novel) of the pursuit of romantic illusions at the bitter price of inevitable disenchantment.

Fitzgerald considered "Winter Dreams" (September 1922; *Metropolitan*, December 1922, *Tales of the Jazz Age* 1922) a "sort of first draft of the *Gatsby* idea."[3] Dexter Green's origins, however, are not so humble as Jay Gatsby's. (Dexter's father owned "the second best grocery-store in Black Bear," and Dexter himself is the best caddy at the Sherry Island Golf Club.) Dexter, like Gatsby, acquires a great fortune and falls in love with a beautiful but shallow, fickle girl. But Dexter Green gains acceptance into the social class of Judy Jones because he manages to acquire both education and wealth. He becomes part of Judy's entourage of men—"one of the varying dozen who circulated about her." Whenever one of her suitors showed signs of losing interest, Judy "granted him a brief honeyed hour, which encouraged him to tag along for a year or so longer."

Finally, discouraged at ever winning Judy, Dexter becomes engaged to a sweet, serious girl, Irene Scheerer. A few months later Judy reappears and entices Dexter away from Irene. After asking Dexter to marry her, Judy terminates their engagement.

Seven years later, Dexter learns that Judy, married for some time to a man who neglects her, has lost all her beauty and vitality. For years Dexter, reconciled to having lost Judy, has lived with his illusion of her grace and beauty. Appalled by the revelation that Judy has "fade[d] away," Dexter feels that an essential part of his being has been destroyed:

'Long ago,' he said, 'long ago, there was something in me, but now that thing is gone. Now that thing is gone, that thing is gone. I cannot cry. I cannot care. That thing will come back no more.'

The vehemence of Dexter's response to the loss of the physical beauty of a woman who is no longer part of his life seems exaggerated sentimentality. But the title, "Winter Dreams," suggests that, for Dexter, Judy is the embodiment of his most precious dreams: "Now, of course, the quality and the seasonability of these winter dreams varied, but the stuff of them remained."

There is a dichotomy in Dexter between the shrewd business sense that made him a financial success, and the romantic vulnerability to his winter dreams that makes him surrender "a part of himself to the most . . . unprincipled personality with which he had ever come into contact." With the fading of Judy's physical beauty all his dreams are gone:

The gates were closed, the sun was gone down, and there was not beauty but the gray beauty of steel that withstands all time. Even the grief he could have borne was left behind in the country of illusion, of youth, of the richness of life, where his winter dreams had flourished.

"Absolution" (June 1923; *American Mercury*, June 1924; *All the Sad Young Men* 1926) is a powerful story because of its vivid presentation of the effect of religious scruples upon an imaginative young boy. Eleven-year-old Rudolph Miller escapes the repressiveness of his own life by inventing a romantic young counterpart, Blatchford Sarnemington. The use of the alter ego is intended to emphasize the contrast between the inflexible code imposed upon Rudolph by his father, a devout Catholic, and the innate romanticism of the boy.

Rudolph is compelled by his father to go to confession and to receive communion with the family regularly. The boy is tortured by fear and embarrassment when he must confess to Father Schwartz that he has enjoyed sexual fantasies. Ironically, with the most serious and the most trying part of the confession completed, Rudolph is trapped into denying that he has committed a minor offense. In answer to the priest's unexpected query about his telling lies, Rudolph proudly answers that he never lies. Then he realizes "that he has committed a terrible sin—he had told a lie in confession."

After confession, Rudolph takes refuge from the nagging fear of eternal punishment by invoking his alter ego, Blatchford Sarnemington, who, unhampered by societal restrictions, lives "in great sweeping triumphs." But, Blatchford Sarnemington notwithstanding, it is as Rudolph Miller that the boy feels compelled, because of his fear of his father, to again be dishonest, and then to commit that greatest of transgressions—to receive communion while he believes himself to be in the state of mortal sin.

The story ends, as it began, in Father Schwartz's study. Rudolph confesses his sacrilegious communion, feeling certain that in the hallowed presence of the priest he will be safe from divine retribution. Rudolph is amazed when, instead of the expected religious exhortations to "go and sin no more," Father Schwartz begins to ramble about parties and amusement parks where suddenly "things go glimmering." Perplexed and frightened, Rudolph decides that he must escape from Father Schwartz's presence as soon as possible. Leaving the priest writhing on the floor and muttering incoherently, Rudolph runs from the study, liberated from his religious scruples.

In "Absolution" the physical nature of the characters is in conflict with their spiritual aspirations. Fitzgerald presents the struggles of three individuals who attempt to shape their lives in conformity with a rigid code.

Rudolph, naive and impressionable, is tormented by his desire for sexual expression and the ingrained fear of swift retribution for indulgence of his physical self. To a degree, the conflict between his outer life, controlled by the self-discipline advocated by his father and the church, and his yearning to express his natural desires freely and without guilt, is resolved by creating his alter ego. Through Blatchford Sarnemington, Rudolph indulges his romantic fantasies, while his

everyday self struggles with the problems of sexuality
and mortal sin and sacrilegious communions. Rudolph's father, on the other hand, is a harsh, un-
bending man, who lives solely by his narrow interpretation of the law of sin and retribution.

Father Schwartz, a gentler, more sensitive man
than Mr. Miller, disciplines his body into an outward
acceptance of celibacy while his deepest inclinations
cry out for the "glimmering" of amusement parks and
"the heat and the sweat and the life" he has volun-
tarily abjured. The most pathetic character in "Absolution" is Father Schwartz, who, Fitzgerald suggested,
has forfeited his innate romanticism and sexual being to
live according to a code of perfection which, in denying the body, often constricts the soul.

"Absolution," like "Winter Dreams," is closely
connected with *The Great Gatsby*. Fitzgerald had
originally intended to give Jay Gatsby a Catholic
beckground. Because he wished to "preserve the sense
of mystery" concerning Gatsby's origins, he excised
all allusions to Gatsby's early life.[4] He used much of
the religious material in "Absolution," which was
published before *The Great Gatsby*.

Another prevalent Fitzgerald theme was the debil-
itating influence of inherited wealth. True to his persistent belief that the very rich are different from the
average American, Fitzgerald frequently attributed failure to achieve selfhood to the possession of excessive
wealth.

In "The Rich Boy" (April-May 1925; *Redbook*,
January and February 1926; *All the Sad Young Men*
1926), the mores of the very rich and the effect of
great wealth upon their personalities are epitomized in
the character of Anson Hunter. Early in life Anson
disdains to "struggle with other boys for precedence
—he expected it to be given freely" by virtue of his

wealth. Although Anson subscribes to conventional
social attitudes, his aspirations have "none of that quality which is variously known as 'idealism' or 'illusion.' " Anson lives according to the pragmatism of
the very wealthy, accepting without reservation the
world of high finance and high extravagance, of divorce and dissipation, of snobbery and of privilege:
"Most of our lives end as a compromise—it was as a
compromise that his life began."

The story proper begins in the summer of 1917
when Anson Hunter, just out of Yale, meets Paula
Legendre, "a dark serious beauty" who is enormously
popular. Although Paula and Anson are both indepen-
dently wealthy and very much in love, Anson is hesitant about announcing their engagement. Before Paula
can implement her plan to force the issue, Anson
becomes inebriated and upsets Paula and her mother.
Although Paula forgives this first manifestation of
Anson's hedonism, they drift apart in the next few
years when Anson shows no inclination toward marriage. Finally, Paula announces her engagement to
Lowell Thayer, and Anson, once again, turns to whiskey for comfort.

His next involvement is with Dolly Karger, who,
in contrast to Paula, is "slackly and indiscreetly wild."
Dolly's flagrant attempts to compromise Anson into
marrying her fail. On two separate occasions, when
seduction seems imminent—the first in Anson's bedroom, the second in his cousin's country estate—the
picture of Paula Legendre that happens to be hanging
on the wall of each room makes Anson turn away
from the flirtatious Dolly.

After Dolly's sudden marriage to another man,
Anson begins to "take a vicarious pleasure in happy
marriages, and to be inspired to an almost equally
pleasant melancholy by those that went astray."

When Anson learns of Paula's divorce and im-

mediate remarriage to another Bostonian, Anson
proposes various reasons why he should not get married himself. Finally he decides in favor of marriage as
an institution and deliberately chooses a New York
girl of his own social standing, determined to marry
without the involvement of romantic love.

At this time Anson is shaken by recurrent rumors
that his Uncle Robert's wife, Edna, is "involved with a
dissolute man named Cary Sloane." Anson breaks up
the affair, Cary Sloane commits suicide, and Uncle
Robert, believing his wife's distorted version of the
incident, refuses to admit Anson to his home.

Anson now rejects the thought of marriage alto-
gether, and, at thirty, finds himself single and lonely.
On the wedding day of his last unmarried friend, the
dispirited Anson accidentally meets Paula Legendre,
now Mrs. Peter Hagerty, in the lobby of his hotel.
Paula, pregnant and very happy in her present marriage, invites Anson for dinner. At the Hagerty home
Anson witnesses the joy of a good marriage. Paula's
happiness is dramatized in a beautifully understated
scene in which Peter tenderly carries his pregnant
wife up the stairs to bed.

After this visit Anson, cognizant of the warmth
and love he has forfeited in Paula, slips into an acute
depression that extends into his business activities.
Upon the insistence of the older members of his firm
who miss "the lift of his vital presence," Anson decides to go abroad. Three days before he leaves, Paula
dies in childbirth. On board the ship, Anson, sup-
pressing all emotion, again turns to alcohol for support. True to form, he attempts to maintain his
irresponsible attitude toward women by starting a new
round of flirtatious episodes. The story ends, as it
began, with Anson capitalizing upon the jovial charm
that most people have hitherto found irresistible.

The narrator of "The Rich Boy," identified only as Anson's college friend, concludes:

I don't think he was ever happy unless some one was in love with him, responding to him like filings to a magnet, helping him to explain himself, promising him something. What it was I do not know. Perhaps they promised that there would always be women in this world who would spend their brightest, freshest, rarest hours to nurse and protect that superiority he cherished in his heart.

"The Rich Boy" is a fine example of Fitzgerald's mature work, in which he displays good control over his style and material. Fitzgerald worked carefully on "The Rich Boy" for about five months, intending the story to be one of his best pieces of work. The only flaw in "The Rich Boy" is Fitzgerald's rather inept handling of the observer-narrator. There are long passages in which the narrator as character disappears and the story evolves in simple narrative form. Since the narrator, as a character, is not essential to the development of the plot, the events of "The Rich Boy" could have been told just as effectively from the point of an uninvolved, omniscient, third-person narrator. After Fitzgerald's masterful presentation of Nick Carraway as narrator-character in *The Great Gatsby*, it is surprising that he is unsuccessful with a similar device in "The Rich Boy."

Hollywood provided Fitzgerald with some of the themes of his stories of the 1930s. The young idealist, caught up in the tawdry intrigues of Hollywood, becomes one of his favorite considerations, looking forward to its most extended presentation in *The Last Tycoon*.

"Crazy Sunday" (January 1932; *American Mercury* 1932; *Taps at Reveille* 1935) is the best of the

Hollywood stories. With his usual flair for making the social metier an integral part of his plots, Fitzgerald presents the distorted moral values of the Hollywood set in three dramatic scenes. In "Crazy Sunday" the artificiality of the movie screen is translated into the private lives of the characters.

The plot centers around three episodes that take place on three consecutive Sundays, with each incident becoming crazier than the last.

The principals involved in the "Crazy Sunday" episodes are Joel Coles, a promising young scriptwriter who has not yet been "broken" by Hollywood; Miles Calman, one of Hollywood's most creative directors; and Stella Walker, Calman's wife, a beautiful actress who has achieved stardom under the tutelage of her husband.

On the first Sunday, at a party given at the Calman home, Joel, who is deeply attracted to Stella, tries too hard to impress the Calmans. He makes a fool of himself by attempting an amateurish performance that fails to amuse his audience of Hollywood professionals. Believing that his career is irretrievably compromised, Joel is surprised to receive another invitation from Stella for the following Sunday.

In the second episode Fitzgerald shifts his focus to Miles Calman, a man who is brilliant in his profession but childishly incompetent in handling his personal affairs. This Sunday reveals that Miles finds it necessary to have a mistress even though he is in love with Stella and paranoically jealous of her. Despite Stella's apparently genuine grief at Miles's infidelity, Joel reflects that he "did not quite believe in picture actresses' grief." Joel's insight that Stella "hover[s] somewhere between the realest of realities and the most blatant of impersonations" does not prevent his falling in love with her.

The third and most dramatic episode occurs when

Joel escorts Stella home from a theater party. Joel is in the Calman home with Stella when she receives the news that Miles has been killed in a plane crash.

In a final grotesque scene Stella attempts to deny the fact of Miles's death by begging Joel to spend the night with her, calculating, as Joel realizes, that "if he betrayed Miles she would be keeping him alive—for if he were really dead how could he be betrayed?"

Refusing to be part of such a crazy scheme, Joel leaves the Calman home. His sense of decency and justice motivates him to reject, for the moment, all that the glittering Stella symbolizes. But Joel realizes with bitterness that the surface glamor of Hollywood has "broken" him, and that, eventually, he will return to its "damn wilderness" and to Stella.

The theme of "emotional bankruptcy" becomes another of Fitzgerald's abiding preoccupations in the 1930s. "Family in the Wind" and "Babylon Revisited" are both concerned with the depletion of moral or physical energies caused by unrestrained drinking. These stories also explore another Fitzgerald consideration of this period: the middle-aged man who seeks to recapture the innocence of youth through his love for a young girl.

"Family in the Wind" (April 1932; *Saturday Evening Post* 4 June 1932; *Taps at Reveille* 1935) is atypical Fitzgerald in its setting and cultural atmosphere. The story presents the struggle for survival among the poor farmers of a rural Alabama town. The luxuriant sprawling plantations of the southern aristocracy are gone, "the proud pillars yielding to poverty, rot and rain." The inhabitants of the area are humble folk, wresting their sustenance from "thin and withered" cotton fields.

By his own efforts, Forrest Janney, the principal character, has risen above his class and obtained his medical degree. Like Dick Diver in *Tender Is the Night*, Forrest Janney becomes a successful doctor. Like Diver, Janney abandons his practice and finds refuge in a small town. But, whereas *Tender Is the Night* explores the causes of Diver's decline, "Family in the Wind" presents Janney at the nadir of his professional life, part-owner of the local pharmacy, practicing medicine "only when sorely needed."

The one measure of comfort in Janney's blighted life had been his love for Mary Dekker: "He had not told [her] how he felt about her; never intended to—she was seventeen, he was forty-five, and he no longer dealt in futures." When Mary runs off with Pinky Janney and later dies from starvation and exposure, Forrest holds his ne'er-do-well nephew responsible for her death.

These events are all revealed in retrospect—the story proper begins with Doctor Janney's refusal to operate on the dying Pinky who has been shot in the head during a brawl. The ensuing family conflict is effectively rendered in crisp, swift-moving dialogue. The tensions that have been developing through the years erupt in a dramatic confrontation among the members of the family: Gene Janney, an unassuming farmer, solicitous for his son, yet quietly deferential to his brother because of Forrest's superior education; his distraught wife, Rose, fiercely maternal, alternating between furious condemnation of Forrest's refusal and broken pleadings for his help; their truculent son, Butch, grimly protective of his mother, threatening to kill his uncle unless he operates on Pinky.

Forrest Janney is aroused from his apathy when a tornado strikes the town of Bending. He briskly directs the emergency measures. Finding Pinky Janney among the wounded, Forrest overcomes his resentment, and performs the operation in a futile effort to save a human life, however derelict.

The immediate agent of Forrest Janney's redemption is eight-year-old Helen Kilrain, a little girl with a pet cat who is introduced briefly at the beginning of the story. When Forrest learns that Helen has been left homeless and fatherless by the tornado, his protective instincts are aroused. "Family in the Winds" ends with Janney on his way to Montgomery to reestablish his practice and start a new life. He gives up his liquor and vows that the "winds of the world" will not "touch Helen again—if he could help it."

"Family in the Wind" is a notable story, penetrating and well-designed. The description of the tornado —of the ravaging forces of nature, awesome and "definite as a pagan god"—is brilliant. The fury of the wind quells the most violent of human emotions, and exposes the pitiful vulnerability of the townspeople of Bending; yet, it also energizes their unconquerable resilience. Through Forrest Janney's resolution to care for Helen and her kitten, Fitzgerald was suggesting that perhaps "emotional bankruptcy" is not always irreversible; that perhaps atonement may be effected through an innocent, giving love.

In "Babylon Revisited" (December 1930; *Post* February 21, 1931; *Taps at Reveille* 1935), Fitzgerald draws on a biblical source for his title. The inhabitants of the Old Testament city of Babylon were notorious for their licentiousness. Many of the Jews—held captive in Babylon for seventy years—were seduced by the sinful allure of Babylon, and turned from the observance of the Mosaic law to the worship of Babylonian idols.

The setting of "Babylon Revisited" is Paris (considered by Fitzgerald a modern Babylon in those days of unrestrained revelry just before the American stock market crash in 1929).

Using a frame device, Fitzgerald begins and ends

the story in the Ritz bar—a popular haunt of wealthy Americans before the crash. Charlie Wales, one of its former habitués, has returned to Paris to visit his daughter, Honoria, who is living with her aunt and uncle, Marion and Lincoln Peters.

As the story unfolds it is revealed that Charlie Wales had left Paris, nearly two years before, after the death of his wife Helen. Reduced to poverty by the stock-market crash, and sick from excessive drinking, Charlie had relinquished custody of Honoria to his wife's sister Marion. He had then gone to Prague, where he controlled his drinking and worked hard at recouping his financial losses.

When the story proper begins, Charlie, wealthy once again, returns to Paris to regain custody of Honoria and begin a stable family life for both of them in Prague. Charlie is determined to have Honoria while she is still young enough to be formed by her father. "If we wait much longer," he pleads with the hostile Marion, "I'll lose Honoria's childhood and my chance for a home."

Charlie adopts the "chastened attitude of a re-formed sinner," repeatedly assuring Marion that he now takes only one drink a day. "It's a sort of stunt I set myself," he explains. "It keeps the matter in pro-portion." Despite her dislike of her brother-in-law (she blames him for her sister's death), Marion is about to relent and permit Honoria to go to Prague with Charlie. At this crucial moment two of Charlie's former cronies, Duncan Schaeffer and Lorraine Quarr-les, both obviously drunk, arrive unannounced at the Peters' apartment. Marion is repelled by the appearance of Charlie's inebriated friends. Fearful that Charlie may lapse into his former dissipation, Marion refuses to give up custody of Honoria. Her husband tells Charlie to wait another six months before he makes another attempt to persuade Marion.

The story ends at the Ritz bar. Despite his sorrow, Charlie, determined to prove his self-control, has his one daily whiskey and refuses the barman's attempt to refill his glass.

"They couldn't make him pay forever," Charlie declares, certain that Helen "wanted Honoria to be with him." But Marion, resentful and suspicious, may just make him pay forever. Or at least until it is too late to make Honoria truly his own daughter, "before she crystallized utterly" into a counterpart of Marion.

Charlie's purgation is far from over. There are so many subtle hints in the story that Charlie is not completely exorcised of his old life. He has experienced the fearful consequences of his former corruption. Yet he comments: "But it was nice while it lasted." His first stop in Paris is at the Ritz bar where he inquires after his old friends. Learning that Duncan Schaeffer is in town, he foolishly tells the barman to give Duncan the Peters' address. Although he does not wish to become involved again with Lorraine Quarrles, he feels her "passionate, provocative attraction."

The demons of Charlie's past are reluctant to release their hold upon him. As he rides through the streets of Paris, he notices that the lurid "fire-red, gas-blue, ghost-green signs" (perhaps of former haunts) are somewhat obscured by the "tranquil rain." But, nonetheless, they are still there—vivid reminders of the old days—just as Duncan and Lorraine are there, ghosts from the past to haunt his present.

Money, conceived as a corrosive power, is one of the principal themes of "Babylon Revisited." Its evil influence is obvious in the wasted lives of Charlie Wales and his friends. More subtle, however, is the deleterious effect that the desire for money has had upon the Peters' family. Marion Peters' self-righteous, moralistic stance in reality cloaks her invidious resentment of Charlie's wealth. And Lincoln Peters, humiliated by his own failure to make money, caters to his wife's whims even though he admits the justice of Charlie's claim to Honoria.

Fitzgerald expands the money theme in one of the finest features of "Babylon Revisited"—its brilliant evocation of place. The Paris of the present, which belongs once again to the Parisians, is juxtaposed with the Paris of the past, ruled in spirit by wealthy American expatriates. In the past Americans were "a sort of royalty, almost infallible, with a sort of magic around us," reminisces Charlie. Paris was their Babylon for American worshipers of mammon. The Parisians, seduced by American money, paid tribute to American "royalty" by catering to their basest sensual demands: illicit sex, drugs, and alcohol.

American money endowed one with a false sense of omnipotence in those days. Even the "snow of twenty-nine wasn't real snow" for the power-drunk Americans. "If you didn't want it to be snow you just paid some money." But the guilt-ridden Charlie, who had locked his wife out of their house in a snowstorm, knows now that the laws of nature are impervious to man's pitiful bribes. The snow of 1929 had weakened Helen's resistance and ultimately caused her death from heart failure. And Marion's bitterness toward Charlie has solidified into a frigid hatred that Charlie's money cannot dissolve. The snow of 1929 had cost Charlie a bitter price: his wife and his child.

The motifs of sin, guilt, and retribution are also associated, in the story, with the exaggerated emphasis placed upon money by its characters. Charlie remembers how he had spent money recklessly:

It had been given, even the most wildly squandered sum, as an offering to destiny that he might not remember the things most worth remembering, the things that now he would aways remember—his child taken from his control, his wife escaped to a grave in Vermont.

Charlie's sinfulness is handled with admirable restraint by Fitzgerald. Although he admits to his delinquency toward his wife and child, Charlie does not wallow in maudlin expressions of remorse. He has sinned, he has repented. As a token of forgiveness—both from Helen and from Marion—Charlie wants Honoria. But Charlie's reform must go beyond the external order he has imposed upon his life. He is seeking salvation through the innocent Honoria. Salvation, however, is a personal matter. It remains for him to reclaim his vanquished manhood.

"Babylon Revisited" is Fitzgerald's masterpiece of short fiction. The story is perfect in plot, tone, atmosphere, dialogue, and characterization. Its thematic complexity is superbly interwoven with plot and structure. With good reason "Babylon Revisited" ranks high among the finest short stories of the twentieth century.

Fitzgerald turned out short stories with a staggering prolixity. He published one hundred sixty stories between 1919 and 1939. Some of them were merely hack work; he disclaimed them himself as "cheap junk," written for the slick magazines for purely commercial purposes. Many others, he admitted, were of inferior quality, but he included them in the collections because he was certain of an appreciative audience among the college set.

There are, however, as we have seen, a handful of outstanding stories, even in the earliest collections, that have the brilliance and polish of his best fiction. For these stories, alone, Fitzgerald merits his reputation as one of the foremost of American short story writers.

7

~~~~~~

Hollywood Revisited:
The Last Tycoon

Fitzgerald's last, unfinished work, *The Last Tycoon* (1940, published 1941), might well have developed into his finest novel. But any analysis of the work is unfortunately delimited by the fact that Fitzgerald had completed only six of the nine chapters projected in his outline when he died suddenly in 1940.

The version edited by Edmund Wilson (1941) includes the fragment, Fitzgerald's outline for the entire novel, and copious notes and drafts that he was considering for its completion. In his foreword Wilson notes that the manuscript "represents that point in the artist's work where he had assembled and organized his material and acquired a firm grasp of his theme, but has not yet brought it finally into focus."[1]

Although Fitzgerald's notes indicate his intention of revising even the first six completed chapters, he was generally pleased with the work in progress:

There's nothing that worries me in the novel, nothing that seems uncertain. Unlike *Tender Is the Night*, it is not the story of deterioration—it is not depressing and not morbid in spite of the tragic ending. If one book could ever be 'like' another, I should say it is more 'like' *The Great Gatsby* than any other of my books. But I hope it will be entirely different—I hope it will be something new, arouse new emotions, perhaps even a new way of looking at certain phenomenon. I have set it safely in a period of five years ago to obtain detachment, but now that Europe is tumbling about our ears this also seems to be for the best. It is an escape into a lavish, romantic past that perhaps will not come again into our time.[2]

The setting of *The Last Tycoon* is Hollywood. One of the major preoccupations of the novel is the decline of the power of the superstar Hollywood magnates. The title, *The Last Tycoon*, enunciates the principal themes of the novel. In proclaiming his protagonist, Monroe Stahr, a "tycoon," Fitzgerald goes beyond the currently accepted interpretation of "tycoon" as a powerful industrialist to its root meaning in its language of origin. In Japanese, the tycoon is the shogun, the absolute leader of the army upon whose decisions depends victory or defeat.

The unrestricted power of the Monroe Stahrs controlled Hollywood through the first half of the 1930s. *The Last Tycoon* is set in the last halcyon period before Hollywood felt the impact of anarchic labor movements. When the novel begins, Monroe Stahr is still regarded by his men "like the Emperor and the Old Guard. There is no world so but it has its heroes, and Stahr was the hero."

But *The Last Tycoon*, despite its rich engrossing evocation of a glittering Hollywood era, was not intended by Fitzgerald to be a novel about the film industry. In fact, he insisted that it was "distinctly *not* about Hollywood."[3] The manuscript and the outline indicate, however, that, in a very large sense, the novel distinctly *is* about Hollywood. In the earlier stages of writing, Fitzgerald obviously planned to keep the Hollywood setting subsidiary to the presentation of his protagonist, Monroe Stahr, who would have been a "tycoon," a leader of men in any circumstances or environment.

The story of *The Last Tycoon* is presented through the perception of Cecilia Brady, a twenty-year-old college senior, who is the daughter of Monroe's partner Pat Brady. The first chapter introduces several members of the film colony—Cecilia, Monroe Stahr, Manny Schwartz, a producer who is no longer successful, and Wylie White, a scriptwriter—all passengers, traveling separately on a plane en route to Hollywood.

Manny is depressed because he has been rebuffed during the flight by a mysterious Mr. Smith. When a storm grounds the plane in Nashville, Tennessee, for several hours, Wylie volunteers to take Cecilia and Manny to visit the Hermitage, home of Andrew Jackson. Even though they are unable to enter the mansion because of the early hour, Manny appears to be intrigued by the Hermitage. Manny suddenly decides to return to the east. Giving Wylie a note for Mr. Smith, Manny insists that Cecilia and Wylie leave him at the Hermitage and return to their delayed flight. The taxi driver, who is instructed to come back for Manny in two hours, later discovers that he has committed suicide.

In the corridor of the plane Cecilia meets Monroe Stahr with whom she has been infatuated for a number of years. When Wylie asks him if he has read Manny's note, Cecilia realizes that Monroe is traveling as Mr. Smith. For the remainder of the flight Cecilia thinks about Monroe, giving us our first impression of the accomplishments of this extraordinary man.

When they arrive in Hollywood, Cecilia makes no attempt to disguise her love for Monroe. He evades her, however, and falls in love with a mysterious young woman, Kathleen Moore. Monroe's first meeting with Kathleen is dramatic, even for a Hollywood scenario. During a minor earthquake the water mains burst and flood the production lot. While Monroe is inspecting the damage to the sets, he is distracted by the appearance of two women floating down the "impromptu river," perched on a huge bobbing head of the deity Siva. When the women are rescued, Monroe is startled by the appearance of one of them, whom he mistakes, in the moonlight, for his dead wife, the beautiful actress, Minna Davis. Stunned by the apparition, Monroe permits the woman to leave without discovering her true identity.

When he finds Kathleen after a concerted search, Monroe is intrigued as much by her elusiveness as by her resemblance to the dead Minna. During their brief romance Kathleen reveals that she has been the mistress of a deposed king who had taken refuge in England. She has been "rescued" from this unfulfilling liaison by an American whom she intends to marry.

Monroe, at this point, knows that he is a dying man, and that his limited physical energies are being consumed by his work in the studio. He vacillates between his obsession with work and his desire for a last chance at love. Monroe intends to wait one more day before proposing to Kathleen, who decides, meanwhile, in favor of security with her American "rescuer." Monroe receives a cryptic telegram the next day announcing Kathleen's marriage.

Realizing that he has forfeited his last opportunity for love, Monroe becomes enmeshed in studio intrigues. At Monroe's request, Cecilia arranges for him to meet a communist party member, Brimmer, to discuss the labor situation in the studio. Monroe deliberately becomes intoxicated and instigates a brawl with Brimmer. Grateful to Cecilia for her loyal support after his disgraceful behavior, Monroe suggests that they spend the night together. The manuscript ends at this point with Cecilia's short-lived involvement with Monroe: "That's how the two weeks started that he and I went around together. It took only one of them for Louella to have us married."

The conclusion of *The Last Tycoon* has been

summarized by Edmund Wilson from Fitzgerald's outlines and notes. The main thrust of the story is that
Monroe and his partner, Pat Brady, each plan to have
the other murdered. Monroe, after one last fling with
Kathleen, becomes desperately ill. Nevertheless, he
makes arrangements to have Pat Brady murdered
while he (Monroe) is on a trip to New York. On
board the plane, he is repelled by his plan to kill his
partner. He resolves to cancel the contract for the
murder at the next airport. But the plane crashes before the next stop, Monroe is killed, and Pat is murdered.

Monroe's funeral was to be presented in detail as
"an orgy of Hollywood and servility and hypocrisy."
Cecilia reflects that if Monroe were present at his
obsequies he would dismiss the spectacle as "Trash!"[4]

Cecilia, overcome by Monroe's death and her
father's murder, has a complete physical collapse and
develops tuberculosis. According to Fitzgerald's plan,
this was to be the first inkling that Cecilia was re-
counting the story of the rise and fall of Monroe Stahr
from a sanatorium.

Fitzgerald described The Last Tycoon "as a novel
à la Flaubert without 'ideas' but only people moved
singly and in mass through what I hope are authentic
moods."[5]

Monroe Stahr emerges as Fitzgerald's most per-
ceptively conceived male person. A poor Jewish boy,
Milton Stahr—Fitzgerald later changed the name to
the Americanized Monroe Stahr—rises from the ob-
scurity of a Bronx ghetto to the fabulous wealth and
power of a Hollywood mogul. Monroe's formal education is minimal, "founded on nothing more than a
night-school course in stenography." Yet he is endowed with those qualities—natural leadership, financial wizardry, creative insight—that make him the boy

wonder of Hollywood: "Success came to him young at twenty-three, and left certain idealisms of his youth unscarred."

Although he insists upon absolute control over every facet of his studio operations, Monroe is still "an old-fashioned paternalistic employer who likes to feel that the people who work for him are contented and that he and they are on friendly terms."[6] Monroe exerts a magnetic power over his workers. Early in the novel, when Monroe surveys the damage done by the flooding water mains, he is acclaimed by his men as they proceed to work:

Most of these men had been here a long time—through the beginnings and the great upset, when sound came, and the three years of depression, he had seen that no harm came to them. The old loyalties were trembling now, there were clay feet everywhere; but still he was their man, the last of the princes. And their greeting was a sort of low cheer as they went by.

In a superb sequence that Cecilia calls "A Producer's Day," we follow Monroe through an "ordinary" day as he addresses himself to the complexities of Hollywood life. Monroe Stahr, the producer, is vital, decisive, compassionate, ruthless. With writers, cameramen, film stars, directors, and even the studio heads, the "money men," Monroe's decision is irrevocable:

There wasn't even the satisfaction of raising a row about it —if you disagreed with Stahr, you did not advertise it. Stahr was his world's great customer, who was always— almost always—right.

In contrast, Monroe Stahr is evasive and hesitant in his personal relationships. His terminal illness is kept secret from even his closest colleagues. Monroe is emotionally impotent, having "like many brilliant men . . . grown up dead cold." Sweeping away at twelve the lies by which most people are formed, "he looked around at the barrenness that was left." Appalled by the ruthlessness of his peers, Monroe creates a new role for himself: benevolent despot. As part of the script, he learns "tolerance, kindness, forbearance, and even affection like lessons."

Monroe has had "everything in life except the privilege of giving himself unselfishly to another human being."[7] And this opportunity is offered him in the meeting with Kathleen. Monroe, however, chooses to remain in his world of properties and discarded celluloid footage where life is defined by scripts and scenarios.

Monroe is actually homeless, a wanderer in the Hollywood jungle. He often sleeps on a divan in his studio suite; the house he lives in is a rented one; the home he is building in Santa Monica is unfinished, roofless.

En route to the beach house, Kathleen facetiously remarks that they do not need a roof because she has heard it never rains in California. In actuality, Kathleen associates a roof with stability, commitment, and family life. Kathleen's dream of fulfillment lies in motherhood. Reading Spengler with her former lover, the king, she tells Monroe, was "just in place of babies." After Monroe makes love to her, she thinks that the child they may have would be "such a bright indefatigable baby." "But you can't have children," she comments, "when there's no roof to the house." And the house that Monroe is building—in which they experience their first love-making—has no roof.

Kathleen's supposition about the California climate is disproved when she and Monroe are caught in a sudden rainstorm. Monroe lifts the canvas top of his convertible remarking: "We've got a roof." His casual statement suggests that he prefers the makeshift, the make-believe, to the completed structure Kathleen longs for.

In his original plan for *The Last Tycoon*, Monroe Stahr's love, Kathleen, was conceived as Thalia Taylor, a twenty-six-year-old widow with whom Monroe has "an immediate, dynamic, unusual physical love affair."[8] In the manuscript Thalia is transformed into the elusive, beautiful Kathleen Moore. A penniless Irish girl with neither formal education nor social status, Kathleen manages, nonetheless, to be presented at the Court of England. Her exiled king-lover indulges his "passion for educating" Kathleen by tutoring her in the liberal arts and social graces. Through this relationship Kathleen acquires a subtle polish that Cecilia describes as "a style that made you look back twice to see if it were something she had on."

The dynamic love affair that Fitzgerald had planned for Monroe and Thalia is not developed in Monroe's five encounters with Kathleen. They have one sexual interlude that emphasizes the distance between them. When it is over, Kathleen realizes that they are just any "two people again." "Don't you always think—hope," she asks, "that you'll be one person, and then find you're still two?"

Kathleen has struggled up from poverty by giving her body. "A laughing wanton," she teases Monroe, exciting him by her evasiveness. When Monroe hesitates before taking her sexually, she speaks to him "coarsely and provocatively" to stimulate his desire. "I *am* rather a trollop," she confesses. But Kathleen is a mother by instinct, a trollop by necessity, a trollop who begs to be made respectable. She covers her nakedness with a "little apron" she finds in Monroe's closet, and then caresses him maternally. But Monroe cautions her not to "be a mother." "Be a trollop," he thinks as he removes the apron. Trollops cannot demand houses with roofs nor binding commitments.

Kathleen is presented mainly through Monroe's perception of her—a perception that is unreliable because of his own ambivalent desires. At their last meeting, when Kathleen tells him that she has decided to marry her American friend, Monroe decides that she is simply testing him:

He wanted her very much now but one part of his mind was cold and kept saying: She wants to see if I'm in love with her, if I want to marry her. Then she'd reconsider whether or not to throw this man over. She won't consider it till I've committed myself.

Monroe resists her unspoken appeal, promising only that they will be together again tomorrow. Kathleen, however, responds to her own great need for security by marrying the American who returns to Hollywood unexpectedly the next day. The telegram that announces her decision to Monroe reads: "*I was married at noon today. Goodbye.*"

Kathleen is a sophisticated, worldly woman who never loses sight of her lowly origins, her early scramble for survival:

She was a European, humble in the face of power, but there was a fierce self-respect that would only let her go so far. She had no illusions about the considerations that swayed princes.

Fitzgerald expected the relationship between Monroe and Kathleen to be the "meat of the book."[9] But the romantic sequence, in the fragment, remains shadowy and inconclusive. It is difficult to see how Fitzgerald could have sustained the romantic element in the novel without sacrificing the studio intrigues that had become his (and Monroe's) primary concern.

Cecilia Brady is described in Fitzgerald's outlines as a "petty, modern girl, neither good nor bad, tremendously human."[10] Cecilia has been sent by her father, a self-made man, to an eastern college to acquire the polish worthy of a Hollywood princess. Cecilia cynically thinks of herself as a "veritable flower of the fine old cost-and-gross aristocracy."

When she returns to California in the summer of 1935, she resumes her futile pursuit of Monroe Stahr. It is difficult to assess Cecilia's character from her few appearances in the manuscript as we have it. Fitzgerald's plans for Cecilia were much more ambitious than the minor role allocated to her in the completed chapters.

Cecilia serves a dual function as narrator-character. As character, Cecilia is one of the most appealing persons in *The Last Tycoon*. She is witty and charming; the episodes in which she appears are presented with compelling immediacy. Cecilia also acts as foil for Kathleen in a larger sense than just the obvious love situation in which she pursues the inaccessible Monroe who, in turn, pursues the elusive Kathleen. We *know* Cecilia, from the first chapter, because we are drawn into her experiences; we know Kathleen only as she appears to Monroe.

Cecilia is "intelligent, cynical, but understanding and kindly toward the people, great or small, who are of Hollywood."[11] It is through Cecilia that we see the marvellously drawn minor characters who are woven into the backdrop of an ordinary day in a Hollywood studio:

Old Johnny Swanson, a has-been cowboy actor who loiters about the studio. By an ironic twist, Swanson's pitiful situation was to be reversed in Fitzgerald's plan for the conclusion. Invited by mistake to act as pallbearer at Monroe's funeral, Swanson finds himself a celebrity again, "deluged with offers of jobs."[12]

Marcia Dodd, a "faded semi-star" who once possessed a thirty-acre estate. "All spring," she reminisces, "I was up to my ass in daisies."

Jane Meloney, the screen writer who is "as lovable as a cheap old toy. She made three thousand a week, and her husbands all drank and beat her nearly to death."

Pat Brady, Cecilia's father, is "a monopolist at his worst," and "a scoundrel of the lowest variety." He regards film-making as a business venture, not an art form.[13] His interest in the studio is confined to how its success "will benefit his bank account." Even Cecilia, who naturally sees her father in a more sympathetic light, admits

that his strong will didn't fill him out as a passable man. Most of what he accomplished boiled down to shrewd. He had acquired with luck and shrewdness a quarter interest in a booming circus—together with young Stahr. That was his life's effort—all the rest was an instinct to hang on.

In *The Last Tycoon* Fitzgerald planned to use the same narrative device that had worked so well in *The Great Gatsby*. Cecilia is selected as narrator-character, he wrote, because "I think I know exactly how such a person would react to my story. She is of the movies but not *in* them."[14]

Fitzgerald, however, is inept in his presentation of Cecilia as narrator. Those passages in which Cecilia is directly involved convey the nuances of Hollywood life with the authority of personal experience. But, in most of the manuscript, the narrative perspective is erratic. Cecilia is absent from the action for extensive periods, and, then, suddenly reappears with jarring remarks such as: "This is Cecilia taking up the narrative in person."

His notes indicate that Fitzgerald planned to refine his narrative technique in the final writing of the novel. But the complicated plans for the development of the several plots make it improbable that Cecilia, as narrator, would ever have achieved the credibility of Nick Carraway in *The Great Gatsby*.

The Last Tycoon—even in its unfinished state— has a rich thematic substructure. The multiplicity of allusions enhance the narrative, elevating the mundane involvements of its characters to a grander level of participation in a universal scheme. The principal themes of the novel are enunciated in Fitzgerald's choice of name—Monroe Stahr—and title—*The Last Tycoon*.

The name Stahr suggests his destiny. The sound proclaims his role—STAR of an unparalleled era in an industry in which the phenomenal, the spectacular, is the norm. The spelling of Stahr retains the suggestion of foreignness, of alienation, of otherworldliness, perhaps. Is he, as Cecilia adoringly describes him, a luminous being who has chosen to be for a while a superstar among the other lesser stars of Hollywood?

He had flown up very high to see, on strong wings, when he was young. And while he was up there he had looked on all the kingdoms, with the kind of eyes that can stare straight into the sun. Beating his wings tenaciously—finally frantically—and keeping on beating them, he had stayed up there longer than most of us, and then, remembering all he had seen from his great height of how things were, he had settled gradually to earth.

We are reminded of the other great solar figures who were able to sustain the brazen glory of the sun: Apollo, the lord of the light of the world; Daedalus, the greatest of mythic artists who fashioned wings to soar above the labyrinth and fly from the menacing Cretan king.

It is noteworthy that Fitzgerald originally intended to call his heroine "Thalia"—an unusual name that recalls the myth of the love of Apollo for the muse Thalia. The muse of bucolic poetry and comedy (literature of pastoral settings and felicitous endings) Thalia is also the muse of nature. Her name is synonymous with abundance and blossoming. Like her sister muses, Thalia dispenses the elixir of unending life, of creative and physical energies. Stahr senses this mystical power in Kathleen/Thalia:

It's your chance, Stahr. Better take it now. This is your girl. She can save you, she can worry you back to life. She will take looking after and you will grow strong to do it.

Kathleen/Thalia becomes for Stahr his personal muse, offering him new life. But Stahr, with a "perversion of the life force," relinquishes his last chance for renewed life and happiness: "Many thousands of people depended on his balanced judgment—you can suddenly blunt a quality you have lived by for twenty years."

One of the most fascinating themes in the novel, inspired by another mythological tradition, is introduced with the appearance of Kathleen riding on the head of Siva. Illusion, mistaken identity, transformation, are the keynotes of this episode, reinforced by Fitzgerald's inaccuracy in describing the male deity Siva as a "goddess."

Siva, or Shiva, is one of the most ancient gods in Hindu mythology, venerated even in modern India as the incarnation of titanic strength. Siva is associated with the anithetical cosmic forces: mystical stillness (yoga) and cosmic rhythm (dance); with universal destruction and recreation and fertility; with terrible wrath and gentle benevolence. In one of his many hands, Siva carries the drum of creation, in another the fire of destruction. Siva's antithetical movements proclaim that in the Hindu cosmos there is constant flux. In an ever-evolving universe of changing forms, it is difficult to distinguish illusion from reality. It is Siva who is the destroyer of illusions.

Reality is antithetical to Hollywood, a world that thrives on artifice, illusion, deceit. In the episode of Kathleen on the head of Siva, illusion reigns. In the moonlight Monroe mistakes Kathleen for Minna Davis:

Smiling faintly at him from not four feet away was the face of his dead wife, identical even to the expression. . . . An awful fear went over him and he wanted to cry aloud.

Nothing is what it seems to be. Kathleen is not Minna; she is not wearing a silver belt "with stars cut out of it," as Monroe believes; Siva is not a goddess. In fact, the image of the idol is simply a property to be used for a Cecil B. De Mille spectacular.

The world of reality recedes once again when Monroe later confronts Kathleen. When he unexpectedly sees her at the screen-writer's ball, it seems that all the people in the room shrink "back against the wall until they were only murals; the white table lengthened and became an altar where the priestess sat alone." Kathleen is "momentarily unreal"; she is "not Minna and yet Minna."

The illusion of Kathleen as Minna is Monroe's projection of his unconscious wish to be joined through love with death. For, in Monroe, the will to self-destruction is stronger than the will to self-realization. Monroe had not loved Minna until just before she died. Confronted with the reality of death, "his tenderness had burst forth and surged forward and he had been in love with her. In love with Minna and death together. . . ."

Kathleen, the illusionist, will divert Monroe from death and urge him into conscious living with her magnetism. Monroe resists Kathleen because she represents not the death in love he desires, but the love in

life he cannot bring himself to accept: "Her eyes invited him to a romantic communion of unbelievable
intensity."

The actual Kathleen is vital, practical, earthy.
"You've got me in your dreams," she cautions. Her
eyes, she tells him, are "just eyes to see with, and I'm
just as ordinary as I can be." Her physical proximity
begins to dispel the illusion for Monroe: "A vague
background spread behind her, something more tangible than the head of Siva in the moonlight."

As Kathleen gradually becomes a living person
for Monroe, he, characteristically, judges her "as he
would a shot in a picture. She was not trash, she was
not confused but clear—in his special meaning of the
word, which implied balance, delicacy and proportion,
she was 'nice.' " Monroe offsets the intrusion of reality
by relegating Kathleen to the world of pictures. For
the producer functions most comfortably through the
artifice of life on film—through imitations of life captured in celluloid squares.

In *The Last Tycoon* Fitzgerald examines his
conception of the contemporary world as wasteland.
The deprivation of the Hollywood wasteland is cultural. Films have become a bastardized art form, exploited by the Bradys whose interest in the "booming
circus" stops at the box office.

Although the brevity of the manuscript does not
allow for expansion of the motif, Fitzgerald indicates
that the studied opulence of the Brady home reflects
the mass-production mentality of its owner.

Cecilia comments that she selected the "processed
leather room" for the conference with Monroe and
the communist representative, Brimmer, because she
hoped "that whatever happened would give it character and make it henceforth part of our house." What
does happen is that the usually sober Monroe becomes

wretchedly drunk, attacks Brimmer, and is ignomini-
ously knocked down by the communist. Brimmer
backs away from Monroe, astonished that "this frail
half-sick person [is] holding up the whole thing."
Monroe Stahr is the "maimed" king of a decadent
Hollywood empire.

Monroe's unfinished house is another manifestation of opulent barrenness. The "builder's rubble"
around the roofless edifice creates an "open wound in
the seascape." Kathleen winces at the "barren glitter"
of the unfinished rooms, furnished like a Hollywood
set with properties—"some grass and things"—
ordered by Monroe "to see how the place felt."

The sterility of film art is underscored by the
swarming in of the grunion with the tide while Monroe and Kathleen are at his unfinished beach house.
The little silver fish come "in twos and threes and
platoons and companies, relentless and exalted and
scornful." A black man collecting the teeming grunion
in two pails tells Monroe that he has come so far out
for the fish because he dislikes those "moving picture
people." He prefers reading Emerson and Rousseau to
watching films. Films, he contends, have no cultural
value because they have no philosophical direction, no
social commitment. Unaware that he has "rocked an
industry," the man moves on with his rich catch of
fish.

Inspired by the unknown fisherman, Monroe resolves to scrap four pictures, judging them trash from
the black's man perspective:

And he put back on his list a difficult picture he had tossed
to the wolves, to Brady and Marcus and the rest, to get
his way on something else. He rescued it for the Negro
man.

The black man's idealism is contrasted with the
box office mentality of the studio executives. An

American who prefers Emersonian transcendentalism to twentiety-century materialism is inexplicable to the Hollywood pragmatists.

Had Fitzgerald lived to complete *The Last Tycoon*, Monroe Stahr would probably have emerged as his second hero of mythic stature. Like Jay Gatsby—that corrupt naif who is redeemed by the steadfastness of his romantic ideal—Monroe Stahr confronts life's complexities with a vision grander than ordinary human consciousness. Monroe imposes an Apollonian order upon his universe. Its success depends upon his sense of measured control, harmonious balance. "I'm the unity," he declares, and the Hollywood community accepts his dictum:

The oracle had spoken. There was nothing to question or argue. Stahr must be right always, not most of the time, but always—or the structure would melt down like butter.

Fitzgerald's first inspiration for Monroe Stahr was the brilliant producer, Irving Thalberg. Like the fictional Stahr, Thalberg was a legendary figure in Hollywood, the boy wonder who, at the age of twenty-one, was in complete command of a film studio. Fitzgerald admitted that Thalberg had always fascinated him. For three years he had thought of the producer as the prototype for his hero because Thalberg was "one of the half-dozen men" Fitzgerald had known who were "built on a grand scale."[15]

Monroe Stahr—transcending even the legendary accomplishments of his prototype, Irving Thalberg—is presented by Fitzgerald as a culture hero. He is the epitome of those qualities of leadership that are most essential to the existence and culture of a group, a nation, or a civilization.

When Pat Brady questions one of Monroe's inexplicable decisions, protesting that "there won't be any miracles in these bad times," Monroe turns to Marcus, the top money man in the corporation. "Monroe is our production genius [Marcus explains]. I count upon Monroe and lean heavily upon him. I have not seen the flood myself." According to Fitzgerald, Monroe has seen the flood, both literally and figuratively. He has had his vision.

Monroe Stahr is the last of the Hollywood tycoons to be invested with such unqualified authority. Before the studio crumbles in the face of the egalitarian demands of the union bosses, the power will pass to ambitious company men "totally without conscience or creative brains."

Monroe is cut down at the apogee of his career. The reader does not witness in him the moral deterioration of Anthony Patch or Dick Diver; the self-destructive romanticism of Jay Gatsby. Monroe Stahr is physically flawed—a dying man. Only his doctors know the seriousness of his illness, for the last tycoon must be as solitary in death as he has been in life.

The Last Tycoon might have been Fitzgerald's greatest novel. It is sad that Fitzgerald was compelled, by sudden death, to leave what he considered his best work unfinished because he had waited too long to begin it:

I don't suppose anyone will be interested in what I have to say this time and it may be the last novel I'll ever write, but it must be done now because, after fifty, one is different. One can't remember emotionally, I think, except about childhood but I have a few more things left to say.[16]

The fragmentation in Fitzgerald's life is reflected in the novel—the unfinished plot, the abortive themes, the unrealized characters. And yet, there is a richness of allusion, of suggestiveness in *The Last Tycoon* that has an undeniable appeal. The Hollywood episodes are wonderfully vital. Fitzgerald's writing is at its best, its most mature: sparkling, witty, graceful.

The Last Tycoon deserves serious consideration in the Fitzgerald canon. Despite its brevity, the fragment has attracted favorable critical attention.

James Thurber contended:

It is the last work of a first-rate novelist; it shows his development, it rounds out his all too brief career; it gives us what he has done and indicates what he was going to do on the largest canvas of his life; it is filled with many excellent things as it stands.[17]

J. Donald Adams stated:

"The Last Tycoon" [is] an ambitious book, but, uncompleted though it is, one would be blind indeed not to see that it would have been Fitzgerald's best novel and a very fine one. Even in this truncated form, it not only makes absorbing reading; it is the best piece of creative writing that we have about one phase of American life—Hollywood and the movies.[18]

Stephen Vincent Benét wrote:

The Last Tycoon shows what a really first-class writer can do with material—how he gets under the skin. . . . It is character that dominates the book, the complex, yet consistent character of Monroe Stahr, the producer, hitched to the wheels of his own preposterous chariot, at once dominating and dominated, as much a part of his business as the film that runs through the cameras, and yet a living man. Had Fitzgerald been permitted to finish the book, I think there is no doubt that it would have added a major character and a major novel to American fiction.[19]

8

From Broadway to Hollywood:
Fitzgerald on Stage and Screen

The Vegetable, or From President to Postman (1923) is Fitzgerald's only published full-length play. He had written and produced theatrical drama since he was fourteen. But *The Vegetable*, or *Gabriel's Trombone* (as it was called when he began to write it in November, 1921), was his first attempt at a Broadway play.

By August 1922, Fitzgerald was confident that the play was "the best American comedy to date and undoubtedly the best thing I have ever written."[1] Fitzgerald expected to prove himself as a playwright with *The Vegetable*. He also expected that a successful production of the drama on Broadway would make him very wealthy.

Even Edmund Wilson, who was often sharply critical of Fitzgerald's writing, was unusually encouraging about the merits of the play:

. . . I think it is one of the best things you ever wrote. . . . I think that the play as a whole is marvellous—no doubt, the best American comedy ever written. I think you have a much better grasp on your subject than you usually have —you know what end and point you are working for, as isn't always the case with you. . . . I think you have a great gift for comic dialogue—even though you never can resist a stupid gag—and should go on writing plays. . . .[2]

Breaking all precedent, Scribner decided to publish the play, now called *Frost*, before it was produced on stage. By January 1923, Fitzgerald had completed his revisions and changed the name to *The Vegetable, or From President to Postman.*

His epigraph, taken "from a current magazine," announced:

Any man who doesn't want to get on in the world, to make a million dollars, and maybe even park his toothbrush in the White House, hasn't got as much to him as a good dog has—he's nothing more or less than a vegetable.

The Vegetable is about Jerry Frost, a thirty-five-year-old railroad clerk whose main ambition is to become a postman. Prodded by his nagging wife, Charlotte, Jerry admits that, like every American boy, he had also once entertained the desire of becoming president of the United States.

Act I takes place in the dingy Frost living room. It is the night of the Republican convention nomination for the party's presidential candidate. Besides Jerry and Charlotte, the first act introduces Jerry's father, Dada, a doddering, half-blind old man of eighty-eight; Charlotte's flapper sister, Doris; Doris's fiancé, Joseph Fish, a lackluster young man from Fish, Idaho; and Mr. Snooks, or Snukes, the local bootlegger who concocts some bathtub gin for Jerry against Charlotte's wishes.

Left alone, Jerry drinks the brew. The curtain falls as Jerry, delightfully intoxicated, discovers that he has been unanimously nominated as the Republican presidential candidate.

Act II takes place in the White House. President Jerry Frost has inadvisedly made the senile Dada his secretary of the treasury. Doris's fiancé, Joseph Fish, is now the Republican senator from Idaho. On the very day that Joseph is to marry Doris, he is commissioned by his constituents to inform President Frost that if he does not dismiss Dada from his position the state of

Idaho will initiate impeachment proceedings against the president. Dada, meanwhile, has decided to solve the country's financial problems by destroying all the money left in the treasury.

As sentence of impeachment is about to be pronounced upon him, President Jerry Frost reveals that he never wanted to be president. In fact, he declares: "I don't even know how in hell I ever *got* to be President!" Act II ends as Jerry is ushered briskly toward the White House gates by two porters.

In Act III (which takes place two weeks after the first) we are returned to the Frost living room. Charlotte is heartbroken over Jerry's disappearance. He has not been seen since the night of his binge with Mr. Snook's gin. (It now becomes apparent that the entire second act was only a dream or fantasy induced by Jerry's drinking.)

Jerry reappears, unrecognized by his family, as the happy local postman. He delivers a letter to Charlotte in which Jerry informs her that he is well and happy in the work he is now doing. The reformed Charlotte vows to "Mr. Postman" that if Jerry returns she will never try to change him even if he too is a postman:

"I'll be proud of him if he's a postman, because I know he always wanted to be one. He'd be the best postman in the world and there's something kind of exciting about being the best."

Jerry promises to deliver Charlotte's letter to her husband. The curtain falls with Charlotte rapturously awaiting the return of "the best postman in the world!"

The Vegetable was intended as a spoof on American politics and on the assumption that every American male desires to take on the "sacred duty" of the presidency. The play also implies that the achievement of the romantic dream often leads to disillusionment rather than to fulfillment. Jerry Frost, a man of humble origins and aspirations has prestige and power thrust upon him. Yet, he achieves happiness only when he is relieved of the burden of glory.

The published edition of *The Vegetable* (April 1923) elicited several good reviews. The *Boston Herald* described it as "exquisite satire."[3] The *Buffalo Express* was doubtful about its dramatic success, but concluded that the play made "uncommonly hilarious reading."[4] Apparently, the reviewers had detected what both Fitzgerald and Wilson had overlooked: *The Vegetable* is a closet drama. Whatever impact the play has lies in the clever and extensive stage directions, and in a type of literary satire that is more expressive in reading than in performance.

Despite numerous revisions by Fitzgerald, excellent direction by Sam Harris, and an exceptionally witty performance by Ernest Truex as Jerry Frost, *The Vegetable* failed on opening night (19 November 1923). The audience was confused by the dream sequence in the second act and by the unexplained transition from the Frost home to the White House.

It was a "colossal frost," punned Fitzgerald:

People left their seats and walked out, people rustled their programs and talked audibly in bored impatient whispers. After the second act I wanted to stop the show and say it was all a mistake but the actors struggled heroically on.[5]

When Ernest Truex announced his intention of going through with the third act of the play, Fitzgerald and Ring Lardner declared that *they* were going off to join an old friend, a former bartender, and that was the last that Truex saw of them that night.

There have been a number of unsuccessful attempts to revive *The Vegetable* on the American stage: in 1929 by the Pasadena Community Playhouse in California; in 1929, by the Lenox Hill Players at the Cherry Lane Theater in New York City. In 1954, Wally Cox played Jerry Frost in a summer stock production in Massachusetts. In 1963, *The Vegetable* ran for eight performances at the Master Theater in New York City, in a production staged by the Equity Library Theater.

A new edition of *The Vegetable* was issued by Scribner in 1976, containing two appendices with several hitherto unpublished scenes. The introduction by Charles Scribner III suggests that:

Possibly *The Vegetable* was . . . a victim of bad timing. . . . It was not until a year later that the lid blew off Teapot Dome. Fitzgerald's political fantasy contained far more truth than the audience was prepared to take in. But a half-century later, after one near-impeachment and with much useful hindsight, this not-so-fantastic spoof can be experienced afresh. Interestingly enough, it has already enjoyed several successful revivals abroad: in the Netherlands, France, Czechoslovakia, and England. Evidently Fitzgerald's caricature of the American dream and its political system is more entertaining on the foreign stage.[6]

It was not until *The Great Gatsby* was staged three years after *The Vegetable* that Fitzgerald had a successful Broadway play. On 2 February 1926, *The Great Gatsby*, brilliantly adapted for Broadway by the talented Owen Davis, opened to a full house at the Ambassador Theatre in New York City. Harold Ober cabled Fitzgerald, who was vacationing with Zelda on the Riviera, that the play, "excellently cast and acted," carried the glamor of the novel.[7]

The reviewers generally concurred with Ober, praising the play as a "magnificent dramatization by Owen Davis of the great novel by F. Scott Fitzgerald. It affords to James Rennie the most complete and promising opportunity that has come to that young actor."[8]

Brooks Atkinson commented:

Of the several attempts to portray on the stage these restless moderns, whose cynicisms and infidelities keep the
calamity howlers hoarse, none has been more able or moving than 'The Great Gatsby.'[9]

Alexander Woollcott stated:

This is the play which . . . Owen Davis has fashioned from
the fine, vivid novel of Scott Fitzgerald. He has carried the
book over on to the stage with almost the minimum spill-
ing: the result is a steadily interesting play, with a cast
chosen with a good deal of shrewdness and then goaded
into giving a vociferous performance.[10]

Fitzgerald, himself, never saw a performance of
the stage production of *The Great Gatsby* because he
was abroad during the entire period of its Broadway
run.

Owen Davis, whom Fitzgerald hailed as the "king
of professional play doctors," later rejected an offer to
dramatize *Tender Is the Night*.[11] Fitzgerald believed
that Davis's refusal stemmed from "his dramatist's instinct that the story was not constructed as dramati-
cally as Gatsby and did not readily lend itself to
dramatization."[12]

In 1938, Fitzgerald received a copy of a dramatic
adaptation of *Tender Is the Night* written by Mrs.
Edwin Jarrett, a Broadway playwright, in collabora-
tion with Kate Ogelbay. Fitzgerald wrote to Mrs.
Jarrett:

My thanks, hopes and wishes are entirely with you—it
pleases me in a manner that the acting version of *The
Great Gatsby* did not. And I want especially to congratu-
late you . . . on the multiple feats of ingenuity with which
you've handled the difficult geography and chronology so
that it has a unity which, God help me, I wasn't able to
give it. . . . You've done a fine dramatization and my grati-

tude to you is part of the old emotion I put into the book, part of my life.[13]

The Jarrett-Ogelbay adaptation of *Tender Is the Night* never reached Broadway. To date, a dramatic version of the novel has never appeared in the legitimate theater.

The Young and Beautiful, a play in three acts based on Fitzgerald's "Josephine" series of short stories, opened at the Longacre Theater on 1 October 1955. The play, adapted by Sally Benson and produced by Robert Radnitz in association with Lawrence Baker, ran for sixty-five performances. Lois Smith was featured as the eighteen-year-old flapper, Josephine Perry, who had been created from Fitzgerald's recollections of his first love, Ginevra King.

This Side of Paradise, which Fitzgerald had attempted unsuccessfully to adapt for a film version, did receive its "chance for a new life."[14] Thirty-nine years after its publication, the novel was dramatized by Sidney Sloane and produced off-Broadway in the Sheridan Square Playhouse. The play opened on 21 February 1962 and ran for eighty-seven performances. The cast included Paul Roebling as Amory Blaine and the playwright, Sidney Sloane, as Rosalind Connage.

The reviewers generally agreed that the appeal of this version of *This Side of Paradise* was mainly nostalgic.

Richard Watts wrote:

The beautiful young sophisticates of F. Scott Fitzgerald's earliest novel seem the most naive of sad and innocent romanticists today. The dramatization of his 'This Side of Paradise' by Sidney Sloane . . . has a kind of wistful period charm and there is something a little touching about its frank sentimentality, but it is also slender and only mildly interesting at best.[15]

Howard Taubman agreed that:

Taste and imagination have gone into the production of
'This Side of Paradise,' and the new adaptation of F. Scott
Fitzgerald's novel distils vagrant moods of nostalgia and
bittersweet sentiment. But, unhappily, it has not been ham-
mered into a play. The trouble with Sidney Sloane's
dramatization is its failure to bend the materials of the
novel into dramatic shape. The chances are that the task
would have eluded more experienced hands, for the novel
is an evocation of period and atmosphere. . . . If only the
surface theatrical graces were enough to make a play. Even
with so original a writer as Fitzgerald as the source they do
not suffice to transmute a novel into drama.[16]

Fitzgerald found a far more appreciative audience
in Hollywood than he had on Broadway. After the
exceptional popular success of *This Side of Paradise*
and *Flappers and Philosophers*, Hollywood became
interested in filming his works.

Flappers and Philosophers elicited an immediate
response from Hollywood. Metro-Goldwyn-Mayer
offered Fitzgerald $2,500 each for the film rights to
two stories in the collection. "Head and Shoulders"
became the first Fitzgerald work to be filmed in 1920–
1921 as *The Chorus Girl's Romance*, followed shortly
after by *The Offshore Pirate*. Viola Dana starred in
both films; as Marcia Meadows in *The Chorus Girl's
Romance*, and as Ardita Farnham in *The Offshore
Pirate*. A contemporary reviewer, Robert Garland,
commented: "There are two good reasons for going
to see 'The Off-Shore Pirate.' One is F. Scott Fitzgerald. The other Viola Dana."[17]

That same year, 20th Century-Fox produced *The
Husband Hunter*, based on "Myra Meets His Family."
Fitzgerald omitted this story (first published in *The
Saturday Evening Post*) from *Flappers and Philoso-
phers* because he was ashamed of its poor quality.

During this period, a Hollywood producer offered to make a film based on *This Side of Paradise*, starring Scott and Zelda in the roles of Amory Blaine and Rosalind Connage. Scott was definitely interested. He knew he was handsome and photogenic. He even had a beautiful photograph of himself, taken during his Princeton days, when he had attended a dance costumed as a convincingly beautiful chorus girl.[18] And Zelda, in his eyes, was the prototypical lovely southern flapper. Scott found it difficult to understand Maxwell Perkins's objections to the project. While the debate was in progress, the idea of a film version of *This Side of Paradise* was shelved.[19]

In 1923, Famous Players paid $10,000 for the film rights to *This Side of Paradise* and Fitzgerald's adaptation of the novel for the screen. Fitzgerald's melodramatic script was not suitable, however, and the film was never made.[20]

Immediately after the publication of *The Beautiful and Damned* in 1922, Warner Brothers bought film rights for $2,500. Starring Marie Prevost as Gloria and Kenneth Harlan as Anthony, this was the first film version of a Fitzgerald novel. According to an advertisement for the film, Marie Prevost remarked that "a brand new line of slang known as 'flapper slang' has crept into existence."[21] The film itself was an inferior production dismissed by one reviewer as "one of the most horrific motion pictures of memory."[22]

In 1926, after *The Great Gatsby's* successful run on Broadway, Harold Ober was negotiating with Paramount for the screen rights to the novel for $45,000. The silent version of the film starred Warner Baxter as Gatsby, Lois Wilson as Daisy, Neil Hamilton as Nick Carraway, and William Powell as George Wilson. The film, directed by Herbert Brenon, received mixed reviews:

"If you liked the book," remarked one enthusiastic reviewer, "you will like the picture better. If you liked the play—you'll like the picture better. If you didn't care for either the book or the play—you WILL care for the picture."[23]

Another reviewer disagreed about the merit of the film:

Here, on the screen of the Rivoli, one of the very best stories in modern American fiction is offered. Yet, the picture is half way dull, half way cold and uninteresting. . . . The purchasing of . . . good plays and novels . . . will in no whit aid movies unless they are filtered through the mind of a director who knows the meaning of cinema.[24]

In 1938, John O'Hara, the novelist, offered to buy the film rights for *The Great Gatsby* from Paramount. The studio refused to sell. Eleven years later, in 1949, Paramount offered its second version of the film, in sound, with Alan Ladd and Betty Field in the leading roles.

Stanley Kauffman, reviewer for *The New Republic*, recalls that he and Edmund Wilson were the only two persons in the screening room at the first showing of the film. Asked by a Paramount publicity man, how he had liked the film, Wilson replied: "Not very much, I'm afraid." Kauffman continues: "There are lots of reasons why I wish Wilson were still alive, but one of them is to hear his comments on the new Gatsby film [the 1974 version]. It makes the 1949 version and 1926 version before it (as far as I can remember it) look like twin pinnacles of art."[25]

The 1974 color version of *The Great Gatsby* was preceded by one of the most spectacular publicity campaigns ever launched in film history. A year before the film was released, *Women's Wear Daily* announced "The Great Gatsby Look" in fashion. The new vogue was featured in Gatsby boutiques in the major American department stores. Bonwit Teller opened "Daisy" boutiques in its eleven stores throughout the country, and Bloomingdale's sported a "Great Scott" shop in its New York City establishment.

Vogue magazine reprinted Fitzgerald's essay, "Echoes of the Jazz Age" and featured an eight-page spread of "see-able echoes of the real Jazz Age" with on-location shots from the upcoming film.[26] *Time* magazine devoted the major part of an issue to the new film, featuring close-up shots of its two leading stars, Robert Redford and Mia Farrow, on its cover.[27]

During the Gatsby campaign, George Frazier commented: "I know of nothing else in world literature quite like the Gatsby phenomenon." According to Frazier, Fitzgerald, a "writer of magical talent," produced "an American novel that seems to improve with each passing year." Moreover, continues Frazier, *The Great Gatsby* "has its own mystique, an appeal of such increasing power that now, just short of fifty years after its publication, it is influencing the lifestyles of practically all of us."[28] Paramount Promotion Director, Charles Glenn, claimed that the idea was simply "to *Gatsbyize* the entire country."[29]

Paramount had hoped to purchase the film rights from Fitzgerald's daughter, Frances Scott Fitzgerald Smith, for $130,000. The actual cost of the film rights was $350,000 paid outright and a percentage of the profits. The cost of filming *The Great Gatsby* has been estimated at between six and seven million dollars. Paramount arranged to have simultaneous openings of the film in three hundred seventy theaters throughout the United States, thus assuring the studio of $18,600,000 in advance bookings.

The film starred Robert Redford as Jay Gatsby, Mia Farrow as Daisy Buchanan, and Sam Waterston as Nick Carraway. The fine supporting cast included Lois Chiles as Jordan Baker, Bruce Dern as Daisy's husband Tom, Karen Black as Myrtle Wilson, Scott

Wilson as her husband George, and Howard da Silva
(who had played George Wilson in the 1949 version)
as Meyer Wolfsheim.

The Great Gatsby premiered in New York City
on 27 March 1974. Such film talents as producer David
Merrick, director Jack Clayton, and screenplay writer
Francis Ford Coppola, working with a star-studded
cast, practically insured the film's success. Unfortunately, *The Great Gatsby* proved to be one of the
most disappointing films in cinematic history.

A preview audience found the film visually beautiful but long and slow-moving.

Reviewer Penelope Gilliatt remarked:

The stately film has much kindness and beauty, but some
works of art have their truest condensed existence only in
the original form, perhaps. Fitzgerald's short novel could
only be stretched out into this mistakenly lengthy film by
the use of repeated views, shots sometimes held too long
for the matter, tracking shots untrue to the terseness of
Fitzgerald, and explanations in Fitzgerald voice-over dialogue of what has already been fully shown in visual incident.[30]

Jay Cocks commented:

The film is faithful to the letter of F. Scott Fitzgerald's
novel but entirely misses its spirit. . . . Fitzgerald wrote
dialogue to be read, not said; and the Coppola screenplay
(much rejuggled by director Clayton) treats Fitzgerald's
lines with untoward reverence.[31]

Charles Michener observed:

Fitzgerald's 180-page collection of words and feelings will
long outlive Paramount's two-and-one-half-hour melange
of images and effects. . . . Fitzgerald's fable about the ideal-
istic Gatsby's ill-fated incursion into Daisy's rich and care-
lessly corrupt world achieved its complex hold on the
imagination not because of its melodramatic, glamorous
material nor, for that matter, because of any remark-

able psychological acuteness. 'Gatsby's' strange, enduring beauty springs from the fable's immensely suggestive, deeply felt telling, and Clayton has not only failed to find an equivalent cinematic style but has proceeded in a manner that nearly flattens the fable to pulp.[32]

The film history of *Tender Is the Night* is singularly lackluster compared to the fanfare surrounding the various versions of *The Great Gatsby*.

When *Tender Is the Night* was published in 1934, few Americans were attracted by a story about psychological disintegration. Hollywood producers, with an eye to the box-office, were interested only in films that provided the American public with a few hours of escape from the stark realities of the great-depression era.

Fitzgerald decided to collaborate with a young scriptwriter, Charles Warren, on a melodramatic film adaptation of the novel. The screen version completely changed the emphasis of the novel and destroyed the dramatic impact of the causes of Nicole's insanity and Dick's deterioration. But even these concessions failed to attract a Hollywood producer, and *Tender Is the Night* was not filmed in Fitzgerald's lifetime. It was not until 1962 that the novel was made into a film by 20th Century-Fox. The screen version starred Jennifer Jones as Nicole Diver, Jason Robards, Jr. as Dick Diver, Jill St. John as Rosemary Hoyt, and Joan Fontaine as Baby Warren.

"Babylon Revisited" had an even more unfortunate film career. In 1940, Fitzgerald sold the screen rights to his short story to an independent producer, Lester Cowan. Fitzgerald was disappointed at Cowan's terms. The producer paid $1,000 outright for the story and agreed to hire Fitzgerald to work on the film adaptation (to be called *Cosmopolitan*) for $300 a week.

Fitzgerald was pleased with the progress of the

screenplay when the studio suddenly decided to post-
pone production of the film indefinitely. Fitzgerald
completed the screenplay, however. He hoped that if
he could persuade Shirley Temple to play the child's
part (changed from Honoria to Victoria Wales in the
film), the studio would resume production of the film.
Once again, Fitzgerald was disappointed.

Cosmopolitan was an excellent screenplay, but it
was not filmed until fourteen years after Fitzgerald's
death. Metro-Goldwyn-Mayer bought the script from
Cowan for $100,000. Completely revised, it was pro-
duced in 1954 as *The Last Time I Saw Paris.* The
lavish color production starred Elizabeth Taylor as
Helen Wales, Van Johnson as Charlie Wales, Donna
Reed as Marion Peters, and Sandra Descken as Victoria Wales. Fitzgerald, however, was not credited for
the script.

The Last Tycoon (1976) is the most recent
Fitzgerald work to be filmed. Even before *Gatsby* was
released, Paramount announced its plans to produce
The Last Tycoon. Despite the *Gatsby* fiasco, Ameri-
can filmgoers looked forward to the dramatization of
Fitzgerald's unfinished novel about Hollywood.

The Last Tycoon, like its predecessor *Gatsby*,
was presented with an awesome list of credits: producer Sam Spiegel, director Elia Kazan, screenplay
writer Harold Pinter. The cast was headed by Robert
De Niro as Monroe Stahr, the Jewish boy from the
Bronx who became the last Hollywood tycoon. The
two women in Monroe Stahr's life were portrayed by
newcomers Ingrid Boulting, as the Anglo-Irish girl
Kathleen Moore, and Theresa Russell as Cecilia Brady,
daughter of Stahr's partner. The excellent supporting
cast included: John Carradine as Johnny Swanson, a
has-been cowboy star reduced to guiding studio tours;
Robert Mitchum as Pat Brady, Stahr's villainous partner; Ray Milland as Fleishacker, the studio's New

York City lawyer; Dana Andrews as Wylie White, a hack scriptwriter; Donald Pleasence as a British novelist trying his hand at scriptwriting; and, finally, Jack Nicholson, in an illuminating, although much too brief appearance as Brimmer, the Communist Party representative who is organizing the scriptwriter's union.

Although *The Last Tycoon* was a beautifully made film, it was even less successful than *The Great Gatsby*. The ultimate criticism of *The Last Tycoon* is that it failed to live.

When the film was released, Judith Crist remarked:

There are, as filmmakers have demonstrated over the years, countless ways to kill a classic. *The Last Tycoon* . . . has been killed with reverence. . . . So reverential have all concerned been in the transition that all the flaws of Fitzgerald's work arrive intact for screen magnification, with the life-giving prose and the projected polishing carefully wiped away. They offer, in fact, further proof that Fitzgerald's novels are no better movie material than those scripts the novelist himself turned out during his various screen-writing sojourns in Hollywood.[33]

It is difficult not to agree with Pauline Kael's contention that:

The film is bewilderingly mute and inexpressive. Kazan's . . . trying for something quiet and revelatory, but he seems to have disowned too much of his own temperament. Though the picture certainly has promising characters, they remain potential, tentative. There's no impetus, so you question everything you see. . . . The scenes remain scenes; they don't flow together. . . . The movie world that Kazan shows us has no hustle. The characters are so enervated that 'The Last Tycoon' is a vampire movie after the vampires have left.[34]

And, perhaps, Jack Kroll's statement expresses the consensus of *The Last Tycoon* criticism:

What's missing is a certain vital heat, an incandescent fu-
sion of style and feeling, Fitzgerald's gallant pain and the
graceful poignancy of his reach to the stars. The movie has
to round off both in character and action what Fitzgerald
never lived to complete, and it doesn't quite do this. . . .
Fitzgerald can tell us about this vision; the film has to
show it to us, and it never quite does.

One feels ungrateful for not responding fully to a film
so full of good taste and good work. The fact remains that
you want to be hit where you live, you want the 'misery
and grandeur' that Fitzgerald's friend Edmund Wilson saw
in the story of Stahr. Despite our sophisticated cynicism
about Fitzgerald's romanticism there remains something
heroic about him. Lionel Trilling located this heroism in
Fitzgerald's 'power of love,' which radiates from his style,
in 'the tone and pitch of the sentences which suggest his
warmth and tenderness. . . .' This tone and pitch, the ca-
dence of Fitzgerald's quixotic voyage toward the ideal
through tawdry seas—is what you miss in this elegant
film.[35]

9

⋙⋘⋙⋘⋙⋘⋙⋘⋙⋘⋙⋘⋙⋘⋙⋘⋙⋘⋙⋘⋙⋘

Afterword

"Novels are not written, or at least begun," Fitzgerald once wrote to John Peale Bishop, "with the idea of making an ultimate philosophical system."[1]

Viewing Fitzgerald's works holistically, one detects an ultimate unity of theme that might be interpreted as a philosophical perspective. Fitzgerald, as we have seen, recreated his world in his novels. Then, he stepped back from that fictive world to reevaluate his position, and, ultimately, to formulate a metaphysical attitude toward the conditions of his own life.

"I am not a great man," he wrote to Scottie, "but sometimes I think the impersonal and objective quality of my talent and the sacrifices of it in pieces, to preserve its essential value, has some sort of epic grandeur."[2]

It has been observed that Fitzgerald's world view was dichotomous, issuing from his "double vision," as Malcolm Cowley described it.[3] Fitzgerald was both a romantic and a moralist. In the earlier days of his career, he was sustained, on the one hand, by the illusion that life was "a romantic business." But, at the same time, the sterner voice of his puritanical self admonished that the price of self-indulgence was self-destruction. The curious excitement of Fitzgerald's best fiction is generated by this inner tension. In fact,

141

all Fitzgerald's male protagonists, from Amory Blaine to Monroe Stahr, are projections of this conflict within his own divided self:

The test of a first-rate intelligence [he explained] is the ability to hold two opposed ideas in the mind at the same time, and still retain the ability to function. One should, for example, be able to see that things are hopeless and yet be determined to make them otherwise. This philosophy fitted on to my early adult life, when I saw the improbable, the implausible, often the 'impossible' come true.[4]

Toward the end of his life, when his romanticism had been tempered by sad experience, he acknowledged:

I guess I am too much a moralist at heart and really want to preach at people in some acceptable form rather than to entertain them.[5]

John Dos Passos contended that, in his last work, Fitzgerald had performed an inestimable service for the American literary artist:

His unique achievement . . . is that here for the first time he has managed to establish that unshakable moral attitude towards the world we live in and towards its temporary standards that is the basic essential of any powerful work of the imagination. A firmly anchored ethical standard is something that American writing has been struggling towards for half a century.[6]

Fitzgerald's place in American letters is assured because of his narrative talent and graceful rhetoric and because of the poignant and illuminating legacy of his age he left us.

Fitzgerald's fiction was shaped not only by the 1920s but also by the grander, more enduring mythologies of the past. From his first novel, *This Side of Paradise*, to his unfinished *The Last Tycoon*, the reader is led to such larger considerations as the quest for the platonic ideal, the high romantic aspiration, the sense of moral destiny—all of which underlie Fitzgerald's distinctly American variations of man's universal longings.

Notes

1. A DRAMA WEBBED OF DREAMS: BIOGRAPHICAL SKETCH

1. F. Scott Fitzgerald, *The Crack-Up*, ed. Edmund Wilson (New York, 1956), p. 177.
2. *The Collected Letters of D. H. Lawrence*, ed. Harry T. Moore (New York, 1962), p. 234.
3. *The Letters of F. Scott Fitzgerald*, ed. Andrew Turnbull (New York, 1963), p. 503.
4. "Early Success," *The Crack-Up*, p. 86.
5. "My Lost City," *Ibid.*, p. 26.
6. *Letters*, p. 459.
7. Calvin Tomkins, *Living Well Is the Best Revenge* (New York, 1972).
8. *Letters*, p. 477.
9. *Ibid.*, p. 357.
10. Arthur Mizener, *The Far Side of Paradise: A Biography of F. Scott Fitzgerald* (Boston, 1951), p. 188.
11. *The Crack-Up*, pp. 69–84.
12. *The New York Times*, 7 November 1975.
13. *Ibid.*
14. Stephen Vincent Benet, "*The Last Tycoon*," in *F. Scott Fitzgerald: The Man and His Work*, ed. Alfred Kazin (New York, 1951), p. 132.

2. AN AFFAIR OF YOUTH: *This Side of Paradise*

1. *Letters*, p. 323.

2. Fitzgerald called the decade between 1919 and 1929 the Jazz Age. In "Echoes of the Jazz Age" (*The Crack-Up*), he declared: "It was an age of miracles, it was an age of art, it was an age of excess, and it was an age of satire" p. 14. "This was the generation . . . that corrupted its elders and eventually overreached itself less through lack of morals than through lack of taste" p. 15.

3. "My Lost City," *The Crack-Up*, p. 27.

4. *Letters*, p. 323. Fitzgerald described his earlier version of the novel (*The Romantic Egotist*) as a "picaresque ramble" of his principal character through life.

5. "F. Scott Fitzgerald," from *The Shores of Light*, in *Twentieth Century Views: F. Scott Fitzgerald*, ed. Arthur Mizener (Englewood Cliffs, New Jersey, 1963), p. 81.

6. *Letters*, p. 277.

7. *Ibid*., p. 323.

8. R.V.A.S. in Kazin, *op. cit*., p. 48. T. K. Whipple, one of Fitzgerald's Princeton friends, is believed to have written this anonymous review of *This Side of Paradise*.

9. Wilson, *op. cit*., p. 81.

3.   BY DISASTER TOUCHED:
The Beautiful and Damned

1. *Letters*, p. 145.

2. "Early Success," *The Crack-Up*, p. 87.

3. *Ibid*.

4. Plato's works are written in dialogue form. The spirited discussions that ensue permit the consideration of diversified, and, very often, opposing points of view. In the *Symposium*, the various attitudes of the characters are presented in a dialectic that leads to the ultimate expression of the platonic concept of the beautiful and good.

5. *Letters*, p. 328.

6. *F. Scott Fitzgerald in His Own Time: A Miscellany*,

eds. Matthew J. Bruccoli and Jackson R. Bryer (Kent, Ohio, 1971), pp. 333–34.

7. *Ibid.*, p. 328.
8. *Ibid.*, p. 318.
9. *Ibid.*, p. 323.

4. GOLD-HATTED LOVER: *The Great Gatsby*

1. Undated letter to Ludlow Fowler (ca. August 1924), Princeton Library File.
2. "*The Great Gatsby*" in Kazin, *op. cit.*, p. 88.
3. *Letters*, p. 358.
4. From the collection, *Tales of the Jazz Age*.
5. "Handle With Care," *The Crack-Up*, p. 84.
6. Mizener, *op. cit.*, p. 307.
7. *Letters*, p. 173.
8. "Echoes of the Jazz Age," *The Crack-Up*, pp. 13, 15.
9. *Letters*, p. 173.
10. Laurence E. MacPhee, "*The Great Gatsby*'s 'Romance of Motoring': Nick Carraway and Jordan Baker," *Modern Fiction Studies* 18 (Summer 1972), pp. 207–212.
11. The color symbolism is especially significant in *The Great Gatsby*. Yellow, in varying gradations (cream and brown, for example), is used frequently to indicate illusion, jealousy, deceit, decay. The emphasis upon money in the novel is underscored by the use of red and gold. The enormously wealthy Buchanans live in an elaborate "red-and-white . . . mansion" with windows that glow "with reflected gold."

White is used by Fitzgerald in a perversion of its traditional significance of purity and innocence. Associated chiefly with Daisy and Jordan, white is, at best, connotative of vacuity and ephemerality. Nick remarks that "Daisy and Jordan lay upon an enormous couch, like silver idols weighing down their own white dresses against the singing breeze of the fans." White is sometimes represented by silver and, in this example, the colors are used together to suggest not only the spiritual inanition of the two women but also their dedication to corruptive wealth. It is significant that when Gatsby meets Daisy for tea at Nick's house, he is dressed in a white suit with a silver shirt.

Green, the color of hope and rebirth, symbolizes, for Gatsby, Daisy and his pursuit of the ideal. Its use frequently heralds some development in their relationship. The green light at the end of her dock toward which Gatsby raises his arms in a ritualistic gesture of invocation is a symbol of the "orgiastic future" that he envisions with Daisy. But green assumes a degenerative significance as the novel progresses. After Daisy and Gatsby are reunited for the first time, Nick surmises that, for Gatsby, "the colossal significance of the light had vanished forever. Now it was again a green light on a dock." The physical presence of the real Daisy dispels, in some measure, the magical apparition he has conjured up in his dream. After Daisy kills Myrtle with Gatsby's cream-colored car, Michaelis erroneously describes the vehicle as light-green. Thus green, in an inversion of its usual symbolic meaning, becomes, in the novel, a sign of unfulfilled promise and violent death and betrayal.

Blue is the most subtly used color in *The Great Gatsby*. In all mythologies, because of its association with the heavens, blue represents religious feeling (heavenly aspirations), innocence, truth. Blue, alone, is used by Fitzgerald to indicate: a) a perversion of devotion, innocence, and truth. Note, for example, Myrtle's soiled blue crepe de chine dress. The spots on the blue indicate that her relationship with Tom Buchanan is a violation of the virtues associated with the marriage bond. Tom boasts: "I'm the first man who ever made a stable out of a garage." b) a corruption of religious concepts. Dr. T. J. Eckleburg's faded blue eyes, which George Wilson mistakes for the eyes of God, are a grotesque substitution for an omniscient deity.

Blue and yellow represent a corruption of the

pursuit of the ideal. Again, most obvious, are Eckleburg's blue eyes surrounded by yellow spectacles. The symbolism is more complex when it is applied to Gatsby's "blue gardens." Here, the blue and yellow merge to form a perversion of the natural green of of the vegetation. The blue gardens are the setting for bacchanalian revels in Gatsby's lifetime. Nick's reference to Gatsby's "blue lawn" at the end of the novel combines the colors in a sad commentary on the destruction of Gatsby's "incorruptible dream:"

> I thought of Gatsby's wonder when he first picked out the green light at the end of Daisy's dock. He had come a long way to this blue lawn, and his dream must have seemed so close that he could hardly fail to grasp it.

12. *Letters*, p. 342.
13. *The Crack-Up*, p. 308.
14. *Ibid.*, p. 310.

5. PLAGUED BY THE NIGHTINGALE: *Tender Is the Night*

1. Matthew J. Bruccoli, *The Composition of Tender Is the Night: A Study of the Manuscript* (Pittsburgh, 1963), p. 78.

2. There are two versions of *Tender Is the Night*. This discussion is based upon the original version published during Fitzgerald's lifetime (1934). Influenced by the conflicting criticism of his contemporaries, Fitzgerald was convinced that he had made a serious error in beginning the novel in the middle of the action. He revised the novel, structuring it in strict chronological order. This latter version, edited by Malcolm Cowley, was published in 1951.

3. Fitzgerald's carelessness with the ages of Rosemary and Dick, and with certain lapses of time are discussed by Bruccoli, *op. cit.*, pp. 214–215.

4. A. H. Steinberg, "Fitzgerald's Portrait of a Psychia-
    trist," in *Tender Is the Night: Essays in Criticism*, ed.
    Marvin J. LaHood (Bloomington, Indiana, 1969),
    p. 143.

5. "Pasting It Together," *The Crack-Up*, p. 77.

6. "The Crack-Up," *The Crack-Up*, p. 72.

7. Bruccoli, *op. cit.*, p. 132.

8. *Letters*, p. 88.

9. *Ibid.*, p. 570.

10. Nathaniel Hawthorne, preface to *The House of the
    Seven Gables* in *The Complete Novels and Selected
    Tales of Nathaniel Hawthorne*, ed with intro. by
    Norman Holmes Pearson (New York, 1937), p. 243.

11. Sir James George Frazer, *The Golden Bough: A
    Study in Magic and Religion*, abridged edition (New
    York, 1947). *The Golden Bough* (first published in
    1890, expanded and revised in its final form in 1915)
    is a seminal anthropological study of primitive myth
    and rituals. Its principal premise is that all societies,
    regardless of geographical location, pass independently
    through uniform patterns of cultural development.
    Frazer's discoveries corroborated the theories of other
    Hellenic anthropologists concerning the ritual origin
    of Greek drama, and, subsequently, of other literary
    forms. *The Golden Bough* has had a profound influ-
    ence upon twentieth-century writers and literary
    critics.

12. *Ibid.*, p. 3.

13. Bruccoli, *op. cit.*, p. 83.

14. *Ibid.*, p. 25.

15. *F. Scott in His Own Times: A Miscellany*, *op. cit.*,
    p. 374.

16. *Ibid.*, p. 371.

17. *Ibid.*, p. 381.

18. *Ibid.*, p. 378.

19. *Ibid.*, p. 373.

20. Bruccoli, *op. cit.*, p. 2.

21. Letter to Maxwell Perkins (n. d.) in *The Romantic
    Egoists*, eds. Matthew J. Bruccoli, Scottie Fitzgerald
    Smith, Joan P. Kerr (New York, 1974), p. 201.

6. FABLE TO FANTASY: THE SHORT FICTION

1. *The Portable F. Scott Fitzgerald*, selected by Dorothy Parker with introduction by John O'Hara.
2. On 1 May 1919, the trade unions and various socialist groups planned meetings, concerts, and parades in celebration of May Day. Recently demobilized service men disrupted the demonstrations in three major American cities: New York, Boston, and Cleveland. Police reserves were called out to restrain the service men. Violent resistance broke out, resulting in two deaths and scores of injuries.
3. *Letters*, p. 189.
4. *Letters*, p. 509.

7. HOLLYWOOD REVISITED: *The Last Tycoon*

1. F. Scott Fitzgerald, *The Last Tycoon*, ed. with notes and foreword by Edmund Wilson, ix, hereafter referred to as Wilson edition.
2. *Ibid.*, p. 141.
3. *Letters*, p. 285.
4. Wilson edition, p. 132.
5. *Letters*, p. 131.
6. Wilson edition, p. 129.
7. *Ibid.*, p. 139.
8. *Ibid.*
9. *Ibid.*
10. *Ibid.*, p. 138.
11. *Ibid.*
12. *Ibid.*, p. 133.
13. *Ibid.*, pp. 138, 140.
14. *Ibid.*, p. 138.
15. Bob Thomas, *Thalberg: Life and Legend* (New York, 1970), p. 10.
16. *Letters*, p. 126.
17. "Taps at Assembly," in *The Romantic Egoists*, p. 235.

18.   New York Times Book Review, 9 November 1941.

19.   *The Last Tycoon*, in Kazin, *op. cit.*, pp. 130–31.

8.   FROM BROADWAY TO HOLLYWOOD:
      FITZGERALD ON STAGE AND SCREEN

1.   *Letters*, p. 160.

2.   F. Scott Fitzgerald, *The Vegetable or from President to Postman*, ed. with intro. by Charles Scribner III (New York, 1976), viii–ix.

3.   *The Romantic Egoists*, p. 110.

4.   *Ibid.*, p. 111.

5.   "How to Live on $36,000 a Year," *Afternoon of an Author*, pp. 93–94.

6.   *The Vegetable*, xx.

7.   *The Romantic Egoists*, p. 137.

8.   E. W. Osborne, in *The Romantic Egoists*, p. 136.

9.   *The Romantic Egoists*, p. 136.

10.   *Ibid.*

11.   *Letters*, p. 185.

12.   *Dear Scott/Dear Max: The Fitzgerald-Perkins Correspondence*, eds. John Kuehl and Jackson R. Bryer (New York, 1971), p. 233.

13.   *Letters*, pp. 566–67.

14.   *Letters*, p. 291.

15.   *New York Post*, 22 February 1962.

16.   *The New York Times*, 22 February 1962.

17.   *The Romantic Egoists*, p. 74.

18.   *Ibid.*, p. 24.

19.   Aaron Latham, *Crazy Sundays: F. Scott Fitzgerald in Hollywood* (New York, 1971), p. 36.

20.   *Ibid.*, p. 44.

21.   *The Romantic Egoists*, p. 96.

22.   James Gray, *St. Paul Dispatch*, 2 March 1926.

23.   Mae Tinée, in *The Romantic Egoists*, p. 138.

24.   John S. Cohen, Jr., in *The Romantic Egoists*, p. 139.

25.   *The New Republic*, 13 April 1974.

26.   *Vogue*, December 1973.

27.   *Time*, 18 March 1974.

28.   *The Saturday Evening Post*, May 1974.
29.   *Time*, 18 March 1974.
30.   *The New Yorker*, 1 April 1974.
31.   *Time*, 1 April 1974.
32.   *Newsweek*, 1 April 1974.
33.   *Saturday Review*, 11 December 1976.
34.   *The New Yorker*, 29 November 1976.
35.   *Newsweek*, 22 November 1976.

9.   AFTERWORD

1.   *The Crack-Up*, p. 275.
2.   *Letters*, p. 62.
3.   *The New Yorker*, June 30, 1945, p. 54.
4.   "The Crack-Up," *The Crack-Up*, p. 69.
5.   *Letters*, p. 63.
6.   *The Crack-Up*, p. 339.

Bibliography

I. WORKS BY F. SCOTT FITZGERALD

This Side of Paradise. New York: Charles Scribner's Sons, 1920.

Flappers and Philosophers. New York: Charles Scribner's Sons, 1920. Contains: "The Offshore Pirate," "The Ice Palace," "Head and Shoulders," "The Cut-Glass Bowl," "Bernice Bobs Her Hair," "Benediction," "Dalyrimple Goes Wrong," "The Four Fists."

The Beautiful and Damned. New York: Charles Scribner's Sons, 1922.

Tales of the Jazz Age. New York: Charles Scribner's Sons, 1922. Contains: "The Jelly-Bean," "The Camel's Back," "May Day," "Porcelain and Pink," "The Diamond as Big as the Ritz," "The Curious Case of Benjamin Button," "Tarquin of Cheapside," "O Russet Witch!" "The Lees of Happiness," "Mr. Icky," "Jemina."

The Vegetable or From President to Postman. New York: Charles Scribner's Sons, 1923.

The Great Gatsby. New York: Charles Scribner's Sons, 1925.

All the Sad Young Men. New York: Charles Scribner's Sons, 1926. Contains: "The Rich Boy," "Winter Dreams," "The Baby Party," "Absolution," "Rags Martin-Jones and the Pr-ince of W-les," "The Adjuster," "Hot and Cold Blood," "The Sensible Thing," "Gretchen's Forty Winks."

Tender Is the Night. New York: Charles Scribner's Sons, 1934.

Taps at Reveille. New York: Charles Scribner's Sons, 1935. Contains: The *Basil* Stories: "The Scandal Detectives," "The Freshest Boy," "He Thinks He's Wonderful," "The Captured Shadow," "The Perfect Life"; The *Josephine* Stories: "First Blood," "A Nice Quiet Place," "A Woman with a Past"; Other Stories: "Crazy Sunday," "Two Wrongs," "The Night of Chancellorsville," "The Last of the Belles," "Majesty," "Family in the Wind," "A Short Trip Home," "One Interne," "The Fiend," "Babylon Revisited."

The Last Tycoon. Ed. Edmund Wilson. New York: Charles Scribner's Sons, 1941.

Works Published Posthumously

The Crack-Up. Ed. Edmund Wilson. New York: Charles Scribner's Sons, 1945.

The Portable F. Scott Fitzgerald. Selected by Dorothy Parker with intro. John O'Hara. New York: Viking Press, 1949.

The Stories of F. Scott Fitzgerald. Ed. with intro. Malcolm Cowley. New York: Charles Scribner's Sons, 1951.

Afternoon of an Author: A Selection of Twenty-Eight Stories with intro. Arthur Mizener. New York: Charles Scribner's Sons, 1958.

The Pat Hobby Stories. Intro. Arnold Gingrich. New York: Charles Scribner's Sons, 1962.

The Fitzgerald Reader. Ed. with intro. Arthur Mizener. New York: Charles Scribner's Sons, 1963.

The Apprentice Fiction of F. Scott Fitzgerald, 1909–1917. Ed. with intro. John Kuehl. Princeton: Princeton University Library, 1965.

Thoughtbook of Francis Scott Key Fitzgerald. Intro. John Kuehl. Princeton: Princeton University Library, 1965.

Letters

As Ever, Scott Fitz——. Ed. Matthew J. Bruccoli. Philadelphia: Lippincott, 1972. (Correspondence with Harold Ober).

Dear Scott/Dear Max: The Fitzgerald-Perkins Correspondence. Eds. John Kuehl and Jackson Bryer. New York: Charles Scribner's Sons, 1971.

Letters to his Daughter. Intro. Frances Fitzgerald Lenahan. New York: Charles Scribner's Sons, 1965.

The Letters of F. Scott Fitzgerald. Ed. Andrew Turnbull. New York: Charles Scribner's Sons, 1963.

II. WORKS ABOUT F. SCOTT FITZGERALD

Biographical Sources

Bruccoli, Matthew J., Smith, Scottie Fitzgerald, Kerr, Joan P. Eds. *The Romantic Egoists.* New York: Charles Scribner's Sons, 1974.

Callaghan, Morley. *That Summer in Paris.* New York: Coward-McCann, 1963.

Graham, Sheilah and Gerold Frank: *Beloved Infidel.* New York: Viking Press, 1967.

Graham, Sheilah. *College of One.* New York: Viking Press, 1967.

———. *The Rest of the Story.* New York: Coward-McCann, 1964.

Hemingway, Ernest. *A Moveable Feast.* New York: Charles Scribner's Sons, 1964.

Latham, Aaron. *Crazy Sundays: F. Scott Fitzgerald in Hollywood.* New York: Viking Press, 1970.

Mayfield, Sara. *Exiles from Paradise: Zelda and Scott Fitzgerald.* New York: Delacorte Press, 1971.

Milford, Nancy. *Zelda.* New York: Harper & Row, 1970.

Mizener, Arthur. *The Far Side of Paradise.* Boston: Houghton Mifflin, 1951. Rev. ed., 1965.

Piper, Henry Dan. *F. Scott Fitzgerald: A Critical Portrait.* New York: Holt, Rinehart & Winston, 1965.

Schulberg, Budd. *The Disenchanted.* New York: Random House, 1950.

Tomkins, Calvin. *Living Well Is the Best Revenge.* New York: Signet, 1972.

Turnbull, Andrew. *Scott Fitzgerald.* New York: Charles Scribner's Sons, 1962.

Bibliographies

Bruccoli, Matthew J. *F. Scott Fitzgerald: A Descriptive Bibliography*. Pittsburgh: University of Pittsburgh Press, 1972.

Bryer, Jackson R. *The Critical Reputation of F. Scott Fitzgerald*. New Haven, Conn.: Archon, 1967.

————. "F. Scott Fitzgerald." *Sixteen Modern American Authors: A Survey of Research and Criticism*. Durham, N.C.: Duke University Press, 1973.

Checklists

Beebe, Maurice and Jackson R. Bryer. "Criticism of F. Scott Fitzgerald: A Selected Checklist." *Modern Fiction Studies*, 82–94, Spring 1961.

Bruccoli, Matthew J. *Checklist of F. Scott Fitzgerald*. Columbus, Ohio: Charles E. Merrill, 1970.

Fitzgerald Newsletter. Numbers 1–40 (1958–1968). in *Fitzgerald/Hemingway Annual*, 1969–. Quarterly checklist in each issue.

Books

Bruccoli, Matthew J. *The Composition of Tender Is the Night*. Pittsburgh: University of Pittsburgh Press, 1963.

Bruccoli, Matthew J. and Jackson R. Bryer. *Fitzgerald in His Own Time: A Miscellany*. Kent, Ohio: Kent State University Press, 1971.

Bruccoli, Matthew J. *The Last of the Novelists: F. Scott Fitzgerald and "The Last Tycoon."* Carbondale, Illinois: Southern Illinois University Press, 1977.

Cowley, Malcolm, and Robert Cowley. *Fitzgerald and the Jazz Age*. New York: Charles Scribner's Sons, 1966.

Cross, K. G. W. *Scott Fitzgerald*. New York: Capricorn Books, 1971.

Eble, Kenneth. *F. Scott Fitzgerald*. New York: Twayne, 1963.

Goldhurst, William. *F. Scott Fitzgerald and his Contemporaries*. New York: World Publishing Company, 1963.

Higgins, John A. *F. Scott Fitzgerald: A Study of the Short Stories*. New York: St. John's University Press, 1971.

Hoffman, Frederick J. Ed. *The Great Gatsby: A Study* New York: Charles Scribner's Sons, 1962.

———. *The Twenties: American Writing in the Postwar Decade*. New York, 1955.

Kazin, Alfred. *F. Scott Fitzgerald: The Man and His Work*. New York: World Publishing Company, 1951.

LaHood, Marvin J. Ed. TENDER IS THE NIGHT: *Essays in Criticism*. Bloomington, Indiana: Indiana University Press, 1969.

Lehan, Richard D. *F. Scott Fitzgerald and the Craft of Fiction*. Carbondale, Illinois: Southern Illinois University Press, 1966.

Lockridge, Ernest. Ed. *Twentieth Century Interpretations of The Great Gatsby*. Englewood Cliffs, New Jersey: Prentice-Hall, 1968.

Miller, James E., Jr. *F. Scott Fitzgerald: His Art and His Technique*. New York: New York University Press, 1964.

Mizener, Arthur. Ed. *F. Scott Fitzgerald: A Collection of Critical Essays*. Englewood Cliffs, New Jersey: Prentice-Hall, 1963.

Perosa, Sergio. *The Art of F. Scott Fitzgerald*. Ann Arbor, Michigan: University of Michigan Press, 1965.

Shain, Charles E. *F. Scott Fitzgerald*. Minneapolis: University of Minnesota Press, 1967.

Sklar, Robert. *F. Scott Fitzgerald: The Last Laocoön*. New York: Oxford University Press, 1967.

Stern, Milton R. *The Golden Moment: The Novels of F. Scott Fitzgerald*. Urbana, Illinois: University of Illinois Press, 1969.

Articles

Aldridge, John W. "Fitzgerald—The Horror and the Vision of Paradise," in *After the Lost Generation*. New York: McGraw-Hill, 1951, pp. 44–58.

Babb, Howard S. "*The Great Gatsby* and the Grotesque," *Criticism*, 5, 336–48, Fall 1963.

Bruccoli, Matthew J. "Bibliographical Notes on F. Scott Fitzgerald's *The Beautiful and Damned*," *Studies in Bibliography*, 13, 258–61, 1960.

Bryer, Jackson R. "A Psychiatrist Reviews *Tender Is the Night*," *Literature and Psychology*, 16, 198–99, 1966.

Carlisle, E. Fred. "The Triple Vision of Nick Carraway," *Modern Fiction Studies*, 11, 351–360, Winter 1965–66.

Coleman, Thomas C. "Nicole Warren Diver and Scott Fitzgerald: The Girl and the Egotist," *Studies in the Novel*, 3, 34–43, Spring 1971.

Gindin, James. "Gods and Fathers in F. Scott Fitzgerald's Novels," *Modern Language Quarterly*, 30, 64–85, March 1969.

Goodwin, Donald W. "The Alcoholism of F. Scott Fitzgerald," *Journal of the American Medical Association*, 212, 86–90, April 6, 1970.

Gross, Barry. "The Dark Side of Twenty-five: Fitzgerald and *The Beautiful and Damned*," *Bucknell Review*, 16, 40–52, December 1968.

Kahn, Sy. "*This Side of Paradise*: The Pageantry of Disillusion," *Midwest Quarterly*, 7, 177–94, Winter 1966.

Lauter, Paul. "Plato's Stepchildren, Gatsby and Cohn," *Modern Fiction Studies*, 9, 338–46, Winter, 1963–64.

McCall, Dan E. "The Self-Same Song That Found a Path: Keats and *The Great Gatsby*," *American Literature* 42, 421–30.

Millgate, Michael. "Scott Fitzgerald as Social Novelist: Statement and Technique in *The Last Tycoon*," *English Studies*, 43, 29–34, February 1962.

Schulberg, Budd. "Old Scott: The Mask, the Myth, and the Man," *Esquire*, pp. 97–101, January 1961.

Vanderbilt, Kermit. "James, Fitzgerald, and the American Self-Image," *Massachusetts Review*, 6, 289–304, Winter-Spring, 1965.

Yates, Donald A. "The Road to 'Paradise': Fitzgerald's Literary Apprenticeship," *Modern Fiction Studies*, 7, 19–31, Spring 1961.